Troy Bobbitt is a retired U.S. Border Patrol Supervisory Agent. He began his career with the federal government in December 2003. During his tenure in the U.S. Border Patrol, he was stationed in both Texas and Minnesota. While stationed in Texas, he performed field work, and immigration checkpoint duties, as the field agent assigned to maintain the station's detection devices, and he served as an interdiction K9 handler.

He was promoted to supervisory agent in 2008 while assigned to the International Falls, MN Station, a northern border station. In 2011, he transferred to the Duluth, MN Border Patrol Station where he served the remainder of his career. Northern border stations are usually staffed with fewer field agents and management persons. The small staff numbers mean supervisors in these small stations perform many additional duties involved in maintaining the functions of these offices. They also work directly with all personnel in the station as well as with personnel in neighboring stations.

Prior to his entering duty with the U.S. Border Patrol, he was an American Bar Association Certified Paralegal for eight years in Minneapolis and St. Paul, MN. During his work as a paralegal, he worked in numerous areas of law, including employment, worker's compensation, personal injury, and 'No Fault' insurance coverage. He served as the paralegal to the managing partner and office manager in his last two assignments. These assignments meant he managed client files as well as managed other staff in the office.

He completed his Bachelor of Arts Degree in Criminal Justice at St. Cloud State University in Minnesota in 1990. Yes, criminal justice is categorized as an art in educational circles, as it changes with society and culture. After graduation, he pursued a profession in law enforcement. At that time, law enforcement was undergoing significant changes, pursuing staffing models more representative of society. These were the days of affirmative action and as a result, the hiring practices tended to favor minority candidates. He spent the next several years working as a security officer and then as a surveillance specialist in a large casino enterprise.

Through a career spanning 20 years in law enforcement, he reported for duty each day, armed with a handgun issued by the government. Unlike the movies or television shows, he only had to use that weapon on one occasion, to euthanize a deer struck by a vehicle. Other than the one incident, the only other time that weapon was fired was during regularly scheduled training exercises. During his service, agents trained every three months (quarterly) with their firearms to maintain their skills. During their quarterly training, they discussed and reviewed incidents and scenarios, always trying to develop new skills and remain flexible in their thoughts, reactions, and observations. Complacency, monotony, repetition; these are law enforcement officers' demons. Doing the same training over and over does not develop skills, it creates patterns.

Early on in his career, a senior officer gave him this advice: "Police work is 99 percent boredom and repetition, and 1 percent sheer terror. You train to deal with the 1 percent when it comes."

To my family, for journeying along this career with me. For understanding and suffering the missed holiday gatherings, birthdays, weddings, funerals, and other special events. For enduring the days, weeks, and months away from home. For the days which ran into overtime, the night shifts, and the 'I'm sorry, I just cants.'

For my brothers and sisters in the profession, stay strong and true. Your courage, moral character, and service is honourable and deserved of respect. To the men and women, I served with, thank you for always being there for me. To those who have made the ultimate sacrifice, I hope this work honors you. You are never forgotten.

Troy Bobbitt

MOURNING BANDS ON

Cultural Changes Effecting American Policing

AUSTIN MACAULEY PUBLISHERS™
LONDON • CAMBRIDGE • NEW YORK • SHARJAH

Ordering Information
Quantity sales: Special discounts are available on quantity purchases by corporations, associations, and others. For details, contact the publisher at the address below.

Publisher's Cataloging-in-Publication data
Bobbitt, Troy
Mourning Bands On

ISBN 9781649795014 (Paperback)
ISBN 9781649795892 (Hardback)
ISBN 9781649795915 (ePub e-book)
ISBN 9781649795908 (Audiobook)

Library of Congress Control Number: 2024909966

www.austinmacauley.com/us

First Published 2024
Austin Macauley Publishers LLC
40 Wall Street, 33rd Floor, Suite 3302
New York, NY 10005
USA

mail-usa@austinmacauley.com
+1 (646) 5125767

To my boss Brent, and the Agents of 'DUM' Station, past and present, and those COs of the MNDNR, it was my honor to work with all y'all. A special thanks to Oscar, Pat, Dan, Sean, Brandon, Chad, and Mark for letting me bounce ideas off you, providing a different point-of-view, and for being my proofreaders.

Table of Contents

Chapter 1
History of United States Law Enforcement

Going way back, law enforcement, commonly referred to as police, is derived from Greek, Latin, and Middle French by way of England. That is a confusing way of getting to a name for a governmental agency but here is how that worked out. In Greek, the word 'polis' referred to a city, or 'polity' by way of 'politia' which in Latin meant citizenship. Those merged into the English language through the Middle French word 'police' which meant government. 'The Police' in England was a civil force responsible for deterring crime and 'keeping the king's peace'. There is much to be unraveled in all the distinct meanings and inferences from each of those interpretations over the years. Let's just agree that the police, or law enforcement, are a mechanism of government to deter crime, keep peace, and maintain order within society.

In England during the thirteenth century, constables were an officer of the court charged with maintaining the king's peace. Constables were assisted by any able-bodied adult male, called watchmen. Watchmen could be called upon to take a turn on watch, walking a turn in a ward and if trouble arose, they would raise a hue and cry. This system lasted for centuries but was easily corrupted. The wealthy and 'socially respectable' paid the elderly and poor to take their turns. The poor were seldom educated and therefore knew little of the law. The system didn't exactly encourage compliance and fair application of law. The language from those times persists though, officers still go on 'watch', make 'turns', and patrol 'wards'. The system was implemented in the colonies too, in Boston, New York, and Philadelphia; it just didn't work even though New York tried paying their watchmen.

In 1829, England's Home Secretary Robert Peel, in response to ongoing labor disputes, and years of suppression of Catholic rebellions in Ireland, convinced the parliament to organize the Metropolitan Police. The force was organized as a military unit with levels of command and uniform issuance. Each man of the 3,000 strong force was issued a numbered badge, a baton, blue long-coat and pants, and a black top hat. Residents of London referred to the men as 'bobbies', after Bobby Peel. They are still with us today in London and throughout England.

Police in the United States (U.S.) has a differing origin based upon geography. In the northern colonies, the cities implemented the watchmen system which was brought over from old England. In the ports and towns, watchmen were charged with keeping an eye on the business interests of the wealthy. The watchmen also kept track of the residents who were frequenting taverns, prostitutes, and gambling. This system really fell apart as watchmen who had been paid to take another person's turn, slept, or drank while on duty. There were also incidents where a person was ordered to 'the watch' as a form of punishment for some offense. If you are a fan of the HBO series 'Game of Thrones', taking the black at the wall. As the cities of the northern colonies grew, the system became entirely useless. In 1838, Boston organized the first full-time police force in the United States. Ironically, the business owners urged the creation of a publicly funded police force, primarily as it shifted the financial burden from them to the citizenry to benefit the 'public good'. They had been paying for private security for their business interests before the police force was organized.

The Southern colonies had a more economic origin to their 'watches'. These colonies were founded with more Spanish influence from the Caribbean, also referred to as the West Indies. Here, the economics of agriculture and the slave trade, brought about the 'watch'. The watchmen were responsible for chasing escaped slaves and suppressing slave revolts. This practice had started in the 1530s in Cuba, extended to Barbados, and ultimately was brought into South Carolina, Virginia, and North Carolina in the early to mid-1700s. This practice continued up to and through the civil war until military troops took up law enforcement duties during the post-war Reconstruction period.

By the late 1880s, all major cities in the United States had police forces. These police forces served the business and political interests of the influential and politically connected. The police helped maintain order among the new immigrants from northern and eastern Europe. The police were used to intimidate and control workers' efforts to unionize. Captains and sergeants of the police were appointed by those in power locally and were easily corrupted.

The police would intimidate or harass voters, get paid to look away from criminal activity or protect criminal activity like illegal drinking or gambling establishments. This practice continued into and through Prohibition.

In the American frontier, law enforcement was unorganized and inconsistent. Federal Marshals had the authority to enforce federal laws in the territories, but nothing else. Local sheriffs in the towns were appointed by the wealthy and politically positioned. The law was inconsistent from town to town as there was no state governance to make laws. Large tracts of land were totally ungoverned. The crowded cities of the East Coast were overflowing with new immigrants from Europe and those immigrants were flowing west into the vast open areas. In California, migrants from China and the Far East flowed in to work on the railroads or other businesses. Gold had been discovered in 1849 and attracted people as prospectors, business owners, hoteliers, gamblers, and laborers. California was also the gateway to the Alaska gold fields of the Yukon. Regions of the United States western frontier were controlled by Mexico or Native American tribes. Native American tribes of the eastern and southern regions of the United States, which had been driven west during the early 1800s, were losing their territories promised to them by the government. Everyone had a gun, to hunt and feed themselves, to protect themselves, their families, their property, and possessions. Veterans of the civil war, used to killing and violence, wandered into the territories seeking either good or evil. The Wild West cemented the philosophy of the armed U.S. law enforcement officer. Samuel Colt made every man equal with his revolver the 'Peacemaker'.

When J. Edgar Hoover assumed command of the Federal Bureau of Investigation (FBI) in 1924, the era of Prohibition was in full swing, pardon the pun. The corruption of the old watchmen system, the birth of municipal police departments in the mid to late 1800s, combined with the growth of organized crime fueled by Prohibition had severely tarnished the police profession. The American public was captivated by novels and short stories about the exploits of detectives from popular writers of the time. Hoover was inspired to make the fictional detective, real. Hoover reimagined the FBI and started to make reforms that would end corruption, create strong oversight and accountability, and result in aggressive crime fighting. Hoover eliminated undercover and local investigative units that were susceptible to corruption. He created a strong bureaucracy to emphasize accountability over the law enforcement officers. He also created educational requirements which led to the creation of the FBI National Academy in 1935. The FBI National Academy extended the reach and reforms to local police departments by offering educational opportunities to those agency commanders as well. The academy also provided crime lab and statistical analysis for local departments, further extending the reforms and professionalization of law enforcement.

In 1929, President Hoover formed the Wickersham Commission to study policing concerns nationwide. The results of the findings led to reforms of police precincts, so they didn't correspond to political wards and separated police command staff from political influence. This effort to reform did make some progress, but as with all change, there was bad with the good. Another reform changed how and where police performed the patrol function and introduced more vehicle use. Previously, police officers had been recruited from the neighborhoods where they lived which meant they knew the people, the customs, the language, and the businesses. They could easily interact with the community members, and they had the community's trust and respect, for the most part. Separating the police from the neighborhoods where they lived caused new problems which persist today.

One member serving on President Hoover's Wickersham Commission was August Vollmer, the founder of professional police reform efforts in the United States. In 1905, Vollmer had served as the head of the six-person police department in Berkeley, California. Vollmer envisioned a police professional as educated at the college level, with an emphasis on management, sociology, psychology, social work, and technology. He saw the police professional working with the community in a service capacity, not as a crime responder and reporter. In 1916, Vollmer helped create the University of California at Berkeley's first college-level police educational program. Vollmer believed police should continue their traditional law enforcement role, however, he thought special juvenile bureaus should be created to handle problems with families and children, that police should be more involved in social agencies, and that police should be at the center of community activities with youth and families. Vollmer, as a member of the International Association of Chiefs of Police helped to implement the Uniform Crime Reports system.

The FBI took over the program in 1930 and it continues to be the principal indicator of the national crime rate and local police department performance. Vollmer saw the erosion of society through the breakdown of basic family structure, church, schools, and neighborhood decline. Vollmer's ideals are echoed today in calls to defund police and shift funding toward social programs and reform police tactics and organizations.

With J. Edgar's reforms, Vollmer's ideals of police reform which were based on social work were abandoned. J. Edgar Hoover re-envisioned police work and administration in a more compartmentalized, structured, and narrow vision. As Hoover's vision took hold, more departments adopted the principles of the FBI. Police hiring practices were modified to base hiring on Civil Service Boards, further reducing political influence and corruption.

Police duties were divided into distinct units of patrol, investigation, and support services. A more militaristic command structure was adopted, moving away from decentralized local management. A principle called the 'three Rs' was adopted emphasizing 1. Random preventive patrol, 2. Rapid response to service calls, and 3. Reactive criminal investigation. This theory of policing continued well into the 1960s. It was Orlando W. Wilson, a protégé' of Vollmer who endorsed the Hoover reforms and the 'three R' process.

Throughout the 1960s, the racial and cultural revolution, civil rights movement, and anti-war protests exposed the faults of this model of policing. With vehicle patrols, police had become increasingly isolated from the communities they served. The rapid response resulted in police being dispatched from call to call, leaving the citizens to crime prevention and reporting. Public interaction became a negative, as police only interacted with the public when a crime was committed, or reportedly occurred. Preventive patrols were targeted in high-crime areas, usually poor and racially divided. This created an atmosphere of confrontation and oppression between the police and the public. In the late 60s and early 70s, the animosity turned into open protests and violence. The United States experienced hundreds of riots and violent demonstrations. Police responded with excessive tactics and force to disburse the demonstrations. The growing medium of television broadcast the events to the nation, increasing the divide between police and the citizenry.

During this time, the U.S. Supreme Court issued many rulings limiting police searches and interrogation techniques. The Court also clearly defined the legal rights of the accused. The Court held in Mapp v. Ohio (1961) that the Exclusionary Rule in the Bill of Rights applied equally to the states, stating evidence obtained unlawfully cannot be used by the state at trial against a defendant. In Escobedo v. Illinois (1964), that a suspect is entitled to have an attorney present during interrogation, in Miranda v. Arizona (1966), that the suspect had to be advised of their rights prior to questioning. All these cases limited police investigative activities. They also improved police departments by encouraging more police training, more police legal education, and establishing consistent and responsible police interrogation and investigative procedures. We'll review these cases and more in a later chapter.

In the 1980s and early 1990s, efforts were made to move away from the professional policing model envisioned by J. Edgar Hoover. Studies and reports indicated that police activities had significantly moved away from controlling crime, to simply responding to reports. Many police response activities had nothing to do with actual law enforcement or preventing crime. Police were being called to handle social issues, medical situations, traffic control and vehicle accidents, nuisance reports of any variety, like a cat stuck in a tree and anything but crime reduction. Police only responded after crimes had been reported. Police officers often had to rely on their own discretion as to whether to arrest a person, issue a citation, or simply advise and warn after dealing with a call for service.

In 1994, a new model of community policing was developed and approved for implementation across the country. Legislation passed provided for the hiring of 100,000 community police officers and the Department of Justice was authorized to implement the strategy. The idea presumably was to concentrate police presence in troubled neighborhoods to create stability and the feeling of safety within that neighborhood. This improved the sense of safety and stability which would encourage the residents to take more active engagement in their neighborhood, further improving conditions. This would then prevent those who could from leaving the area and causing further decline and neglect.

On 11 September 2001, everything changed. After the terrorist attacks in New York, Washington, D.C., and Shanksville, Pennsylvania, counterterrorism became the goal of the police. The local police agencies that had developed effective community policing models didn't want to lose that connection and withhold information from within the community, especially if it was ethnically targeted. Some police departments saw terrorism as an act of war, not of law enforcement. Local police and federal law enforcement agencies often do not share a common goal especially when it comes to adjudication of cases. The pursuit of terrorist suspects involves multi-national cooperation, something local police departments obviously do not possess.

Historically, law enforcement in the United States has its roots in Western Europe but is distinctly American. Having been influenced by English law and tradition, Spanish influences of the Caribbean, the slave trade, commercial interests of businesses and merchants, the American frontier, and the urbanization of American cities, many factors played a part in American law enforcement. Over the last 150 years, efforts have been made to reform and adapt law enforcement to American society. Those efforts continue today, and a new chapter will be written as our society and culture change yet again. Change takes time and we are still determining the course of society with new technologies, new threats, and new expectations of the public. Criminal Justice is an art, susceptible to society's changing values and expectations. We will have to wait and see what new direction society chooses for its law enforcement who is charged to 'serve and protect' that society.

Chapter 2
The United States Constitution

Before we explore the specific components of the United States Judicial system, we should briefly review the construct of our system of national government. On 15 November 1777, the Congress of the Confederation adopted The Articles of Confederation which created the central government of the new United States. Under the Articles, the national government was only empowered to conduct diplomacy, declare war, set weights and measures, and serve as the final arbiter between the states. All decisions were required to be unanimous, and each state received a single vote. The Articles also made the federal government dependent upon the states financially, not enabling the federal government to raise funds, while requiring it to support a national defense. With the limitations on authority and with a requirement of unanimity of decisions, the government was paralyzed. The Articles of Confederation controlled United States governmental structure throughout the War of Independence with England. After the war ended and following several post-war years of difficulties, it was determined a new governmental structure was required.

In May of 1787, a Constitutional Convention was called in Philadelphia, the then-national capital, with the intention of drafting a new Constitution. After a period of debate and drafting, the Constitution was sent to the states for ratification. It was established that nine of the thirteen states had to ratify the Constitution before it could be accepted as a form of government. On 22 June 1788, New Hampshire ratified the new Constitution becoming the ninth state to do so. The Confederation Congress, as it was then called, established 9 March 1789, as the date that the Constitution would go into effect and the new government structure would be enacted. Rhode Island, which did not send delegates to the Constitutional Convention, was the last state to ratify the Constitution, doing so on 29 May 1790.

While the states, well the people in them, were considering whether to ratify the Constitution, a series of 85 articles was published in newspapers explaining and supporting the new Constitution. The articles were published anonymously but were drafted by James Madison, Alexander Hamilton, and John Jay. These articles, referred to as The Federalist Papers, remain an important resource in understanding the intentions of the drafters of the Constitution.

The Bill of Rights introduced by James Madison to the first Congress in 1789, were the first Amendments made to the Constitution after ratification. The Constitution itself did not enumerate the rights of the people; it only formed the government and set the rights that the government possessed. All other rights were left to the states and the people.

Madison initially presented 12 Amendments, of which 10 were adopted. These 10 Amendments, we refer to as the Bill of Rights. They were not initially part of the Constitution but as they are entitled, are Amendments to the Constitution. The next time you hear the phrase, 'It's my Constitutional right,' you can respond, 'No, in actuality, it's your right granted under the First Amendment to the Constitution, etc.' One of the twelve initial Amendments, which dealt with congressional salaries, was adopted as the 27th Amendment on 18 May 1992. Only six states originally ratified the Amendment, so it lay dormant until 1873 when Ohio ratified it in protest to congressional members attempts to increase their pay. In 1982, an undergraduate student at the University of Texas in Austin prepared a paper that initiated a movement to curtail political corruption. It took ten years for the requisite two-thirds of the states to ratify the Amendment, 202 years after its initial introduction. The government does indeed move slowly at times. By the way, the student received a 'C' grade on the paper as the professor did not find the argument that the Amendment was still pending convincing.

The Constitution sets out the Articles of Incorporation which form the governmental structure. The Constitution created three separate, but equal branches of government. It set forth checks and balances on each branch by the other branches to prevent one branch from dominating the others. The branches were defined as the Legislative, Executive, and Judicial. The Legislative branch would consist of the House of Representatives and the

Senate. The powers of each were clearly defined and set forth as well as how they were to be constituted and represent the people of the states. The Executive branch was the office of the President and Vice President, elected by the number of electors equal to the number of Senators and members of the House of Representatives of the state. The final branch, the Judicial, established the Supreme Court of the United States and the lesser federal courts. The Judicial branch's jurisdictional limits were specifically defined.

Articles IV through VII set forth how states will relate to each other in business and law, how Amendments to the Constitution may be proposed and ratified, transference of debts and obligations from the former government to the new government, and how ratification shall be determined and notes a typographical error or two in the document. They didn't have white-out tape or a backspace button and re-writing the whole document wasn't going to happen.

Article III of the Constitution creates the United States Supreme Court but leaves all inferior courts to the Legislative branch to create and organize their structure. The 10th Amendment of the Constitution states that all powers not delegated to the United States by the Constitution, nor prohibited by it to the states, are reserved to the states respectively, or to the people. This means that all the states have the authority to create their own court systems and structures as they see fit. In the next chapter, we'll look at the different components of the judicial system that resulted under this Article and the 10th Amendment that followed.

Chapter 3
Components of the United States Criminal Justice System

Now with an understanding of the structure of the government, how the powers of the government were divided, and how the United States (U.S.) court system was developed, we can look at the specific components of the judicial system. We'll start at the lowest and most visible level of our U.S. Criminal Justice system, law enforcement.

Law enforcement encompasses various names and levels of organization. As we found in Chapter One, it is a part of the government charged with maintaining order and peace and deterring criminal activity. Law enforcement organizations use the terms police, peace officer, community service officer, constable, sheriff deputy, officer, or agent to refer to their front-line personnel. These persons serve in all levels of government from the federal level down through the states, counties, municipalities, and even in special governmental departments or districts. Tribal governments may also develop their own law enforcement under the powers granted to them through under their treaty with the United States.

Law enforcement agencies and their personnel are usually divided into separate divisions, bureaus, or departments as most entities still follow the J. Edgar Hoover vision of law enforcement organization. Personnel may serve in patrol divisions, investigative divisions, and support divisions. We'll explore each of these three divisions in general terms, as there are many variances based on size, location, and governmental organization.

Speaking in broad terms, patrol division personnel are your most visible and frequently encountered part of law enforcement. Patrol officers respond to calls for assistance and criminal activity reports in their assigned jurisdictions. Beyond those duties, these personnel also respond to vehicle collisions, domestic disturbances, public assistance calls, and so many other types of community service that they are too numerous to list here. You can see patrol personnel directing traffic at a parade, providing security at a sporting event, escorting a funeral procession, or speaking to youngsters at a local school event. Although these personnel are encouraged to actively engage in anti-crime patrol and crime prevention, most of their time is spent responding to activity reports. Being called after an incident or crime has already occurred. They prepare reports and make initial evidentiary seizures and investigative decisions. During some interactions, they issue summons or citations, mostly for minor infractions of state or local law or in cases of traffic violations.

The next level in most law enforcement agencies is the investigative division. Personnel at this level of law enforcement are generally involved in cases that have a higher level of importance or repetition. Referred to as detectives, inspectors, investigators, or special agents, personnel at this level take the reports from the patrol division and work to develop a possible referral for criminal prosecution. These personnel work in organized crime, drug trafficking, burglary and robbery cases, and homicides. When crimes of this nature cross state lines or involve multiple jurisdictions, then state and/or federal law enforcement entities get involved to coordinate and assist in solving these crimes. Federal law enforcement entities such as the Federal Bureau of Investigation (FBI), Alcohol, Tobacco, Firearms and Explosives (ATF), Drug Enforcement Agency (DEA), Homeland Security Investigations (HSI), and the Secret Service (USSS) all have specific areas of expertise in investigative tactics, capabilities, and support that they can bring to bear to assist the investigation.

The FBI maintains fingerprint data, stolen property records, firearms registration information, and now deoxyribonucleic acid (DNA) samples of persons which can be accessed by law enforcement agencies across the country for investigative purposes. Recently, a new tool to identify people has started to be gathered, retinal scans. Most states have investigative bureaus which mimic federal agencies that can be called upon to assist in investigations as well.

The primary purpose of the investigative divisions is to take the initial information gathered by the patrol division and develop that information to a point where prosecutors may present a case in a court of law. The investigative divisions coordinate with the prosecutor to determine what laws have been violated, what the factors are that create that violation, and obtain the evidence necessary to prove that the violation occurred.

A very seldom recognized division of the law enforcement agency is the support division. Support divisions include training, fleet maintenance, records management, property management, emergency dispatch services, clerical, and supply. These departments are crucial to the effective operation of today's law enforcement agency. Training is a constant within law enforcement, whether it be physical, mental, or psychological. Training provides personnel with updates on changes in the law as well as new trends and the introduction of new equipment. Maintaining skills that have been developed over time is also crucial, as well as unlearning bad habits.

Psychological support has only recently been recognized as critical to the health of personnel. Psychological services of the past were targeted toward personnel who had been involved in critical incidents. Current efforts are being made to make psychological services readily available, without stigma, to agency personnel at all levels, regardless of involvement. Unfortunately, law enforcement personnel are exposed to psychologically challenging incidents regularly while on duty. It may be a serious motor vehicle accident, a domestic violence incident, a natural disaster, or other critical incident that the employee has experienced. Personnel need to learn healthy ways of relieving the stresses caused by experiencing these types of incidents. Like the military's gradual recognition of post-traumatic stress disorder (PTSD), law enforcement departments are recognizing this in their personnel as well.

Other support division services such as fleet management, records, property retention, and supply are equally important. Law enforcement departments must remain able to serve the area they represent. Without working and effective vehicle services, calls would not be responded to. Those calls usually originate from the emergency dispatch staff. These personnel are the voice on the line when the public calls out for help. They must remain calm and in control, gather pertinent information, relay that information to the responding officer, and attempt to assist the person if needed. As if that isn't enough, they also search databases for information concerning the reported incident and make sure the responding personnel have that information when they arrive on the scene. Records, property, and supply personnel ensure that the proper records are maintained and available for recall, property is secured for court use and returned to the rightful owners, and that the department has the necessary equipment to conduct its business.

When it comes to presenting cases in courts of law, that is the responsibility of the attorneys in the prosecution departments. These attorneys represent the people of the jurisdiction, without prejudice or bias. Prosecutors present case information to Grand Juries which determine whether a case is sufficiently developed to proceed to the trial phase. There are prosecutors at all levels of government, city or municipality, county, state, and federal districts. They may go by the title of city attorney, county attorney, district attorney of the state, or the federal district court.

In most governmental city, county, and state jurisdictions, the leader of the District Attorney's Office is an elected official. The remaining personnel, including the assistant district attorneys are paid staff of the office, hired into the position. At the federal level, the Attorney General of the United States heads the Department of Justice and is appointed to that position by the president. The separate United States Judicial Districts are led by persons appointed by the Attorney General. All the other staff are employees of the federal government.

The attorneys at this level of the judicial system can greatly influence the impact of criminal prosecutions and issues related to civil and criminal litigation. The decisions made here not only affect criminal law and justice but also affect cultural norms and expectations. Criminal prosecutors control which crimes are enforced, and which are not. If prosecutors choose not to bring cases against persons committing certain crimes, say for example, shoplifting, then that criminal behavior is thereby effectively de-criminalized. Even though the legislature has passed a law prohibiting that behavior, the police have arrested a person and the investigators have developed evidence to proceed to trial, if the prosecutor's office does not follow through, there are no consequences for the improper behavior. The judicial system is effectively suspended and rendered ineffective. These persons may also bring civil litigation on behalf of the people against individuals, corporations, or foreign actors. These actions could be for dangerous products, hazardous conditions created by industry, or to compel behavior consistent with law or policy. When these powers are exercised, society and culture can be significantly affected.

The United States Courts systems have the responsibility of presiding over the proper adjudication of cases as defined by law duly passed by the legislative body or by established precedent through previously decided case law. The Courts system encompasses all levels of government from the United States Supreme Court, State Supreme Courts, the various Courts of Appeals, and then district courts at both state and federal levels. There are also courts at the county and municipal levels as well as special courts with specific responsibilities such as juvenile and family matters. The judge presiding over the Court is an elected official, except in the federal system. Judges in the federal system are appointed by the president with the approval and consent of the United States Senate following confirmation hearings. Federal judges are appointed for life terms of service unless they retire or are removed for misconduct by impeachment by the House and Senate. Magistrate judges are appointed by district court judges for specific terms of service to handle certain matters, such as pre-trial proceedings. The courts are governed by published Rules of Procedure, approved by legislative bodies which are based upon common and case law. Whether prosecution or defense, plaintiff or defendant, criminal or civil, there are specific rules that must be followed that govern party and counsel behavior. This ensures fairness, openness, and equality in judicial proceedings.

The final part of the judicial system is the corrections, parole, and probation system. This encompasses prisons, county jails, and all other forms of punishment which may arise from a criminal conviction. Obviously, prisons and jails are maintained for separating a convicted person from the public during a specific term of confinement. Prisons and jails serve different classes of convicted persons, just as there are different classifications of risk associated with the populations at said facilities. Different levels of government operate detention facilities based on criminal conduct and the court of jurisdiction. Some facilities are even privately operated businesses contracted to a governmental body.

The probation and parole agencies have multiple responsibilities at different parts of the criminal prosecution. Once a person has been convicted of a criminal act in court or pleads guilty to the act, there is a hearing set to determine sentencing. There are employees within these departments that conduct investigations which they provide to the judge prior to the sentencing hearing providing recommendations and guidance concerning the possible punishments. There are many factors, determined by each governmental body, which affect this decision.

Different classes of offenses carry legislatively determined terms of punishment. Different persons have differing criminal histories which affect possible sentencing. Different violations of law combined with other violations can result in more severe terms of punishment. Then there is the input of crime victims, families, and the possibility of financial damages which may result in restitution claims to consider. Restitution claims are ordered in cases where financial damages, such as theft or property destruction have occurred, and the defendant is ordered to make payments to repay the victim for those losses. The employees conducting these investigations gather all the information for each case and provide the judge with the necessary knowledge to serve justice.

Another division of the probation and parole department monitors and assists those persons who are released into the public to ensure they meet the conditions of their release to remain in the public. This may be a person convicted of a minor offense that is ordered on supervised release for a length of time, ordered to complete classes, provide certain services, or pay certain amounts in damages prior to their punishment being determined complete. Usually, the person is also required to regularly report to a probation officer for interviews, possibly drug or alcohol testing, or simple checkups. Here the probation officer reports back to the court that the person is either complying with their release conditions or is in violation of them, which may result in re-arrest and possible confinement. Lastly, the parole department performs mostly these same functions; however, these persons have usually served a term of confinement and have time remaining to serve but are afforded the chance to complete their term under conditions of release.

Overall, the criminal justice system is a large team striving to maintain peace and ensure justice under the law is equally and fairly afforded to everyone within the society. Each component works for and with the other components to make this happen. Without the law enforcement officer, the prosecutors wouldn't have cases to present. Without prosecutors, the courts wouldn't have cases to schedule and preside over. Without courts to determine whether violations of law have occurred, the corrections level wouldn't have persons to detain and monitor. Come to think of it, without criminal activity in society, we wouldn't need many of these systems. Wouldn't that be a wonderful problem to have, and to celebrate?

Chapter 4
Constitutional Law for Police Officers

We have explored the history of law enforcement, the development of our national system of government with the Constitution, and the various components of the criminal justice system in the United States. In this chapter, we will explore what portions of the law, duly enacted by legislatures, and as interpreted by courts, directs, and affects law enforcement personnel in their daily activities. There are two different types of law, Constitutional and Statutory. As it states, Constitutional law is derived directly from the Bill of Rights and further Amendments to the United States Constitution. Statutory law is those laws that legislatures of the United States and the various states have enacted to guide our society and culture. The different types of laws each have differing levels of priority and status within the judicial system. These levels of priority establish standing, precedent, and jurisdiction over cases under the judicial system. There is a third type of law that lower governmental entities may enact which are referred to as ordinances. Typically, ordinances are created by counties, parishes, and municipalities for their specific jurisdictions.

A law enforcement professional must navigate all the various levels of law that are valid while they are performing their duties. This knowledge requires education and training. Each state sets its own standards of training for law enforcement professionals. Some require two- or four-year college degrees. All, I would hope, require candidates to attend and pass training academies. Candidates are taught Constitutional and Statutory law, proper tactics and skills for various conduct, driving skills, physical training and conditioning, weapons handling and skills, and then individual agency policy and procedures. No matter the governmental level, training is required. When I went to my academy, it was 21 weeks long. Training and education are a constant and are ongoing throughout the career as laws, tactics and techniques, and cultural changes occur. Law enforcement professionals are always maintaining skills learned and learning new skills that replace outdated techniques.

There is no better place to begin with the law than with the United States Constitution, the Bill of Rights, and other Amendments. Here they are with very simplistic descriptions of what they cover:

First: right to free speech, press, assemble, protest (petition the government for remedy), and of religion;

Second: right to keep and bear arms;

Third: prevents the government from quartering soldiers in a person's home;

Fourth: bars the government from unreasonable search and seizure of a person or their property;

Fifth: serious criminal charges must be initiated by Grand Jury proceedings, prevents double jeopardy (being tried twice for the same offense), provides for just compensation for the seizure of property, right against self-incrimination, and provides due process of law in federal cases (fair procedures and trial processes);

Sixth: right to speedy and public trial and trial by a jury in federal cases;

Seventh: jury trial extended to civil cases in federal court;

Eighth: prevents excessive bail and fines and cruel and unusual punishments;

Ninth: listing rights in the Constitution does not mean that people do not have other rights that have not been spelled out; and

Tenth: that the federal government has only those powers delegated to it in the Constitution, if it isn't listed, then it belongs to the states or the people.

There, a quick and easy Bill of Rights review.

One other Amendment that we should list is the Fourteenth which was ratified after the civil war during Reconstruction. The Fourteenth Amendment grants citizenship to all persons born or naturalized in the United States. This provision guaranteed civil and equal rights to all formerly enslaved persons. Another provision of the Amendment is more relevant to this book though. That provision reads: …'nor shall any state deprive any person of life, liberty, or property, without due process of law; nor deny any person within its jurisdiction, the equal protection of the laws.' This provision was intended to extend a person's rights under the federal court system to the states, bringing the state courts in line with federal court rules and procedures. The Fourteenth Amendment is referred to as the Due Process Clause in legal circles.

We could spend several pages exploring each of the Amendments listed above and how they impact law enforcement. I think it would be better to simply summarize some of the major points from the First, Second, and Eighth before we explore the Fourth, Fifth, and Sixth more in-depth.

The First Amendment provides for the right of assembly and to petition the government for remedies. From this, the American public gets the right to protest. Also, our right to free speech is guaranteed within this language. Now, just because a person has the right to free speech doesn't mean that speech is unlimited. There is an old adage that yelling fire in a crowded venue is not free speech as it may induce panic resulting in injury to others. The updated language refers to saying bomb in an airport is not free speech. There are limits to our right to free speech that are codified into laws throughout the country such as liable and slander.

Similarly, our right to protest and gather has limits. Usually, organized peaceful protests are scheduled, planned, and permitted by a governmental entity. This provides time for governmental planning of personnel and facilities, say a park for a gathering or a street route for a march. Law enforcement can be scheduled to provide traffic control and protection to the participants and facilities provided such as bathrooms and other needs can be addressed to allow the gathering to proceed smoothly and safely. Of course, there are spontaneous protests which occur following events at times. In these cases, protests may be allowed to proceed as long as the protest or gathering remains peaceful and non-disruptive to society. A protest that is declared unlawful by governmental entities for specifically stated reasons becomes an unlawful gathering; sometimes called a riot. In these instances, law enforcement may be ordered to end the gathering for the safety of the public, participants, and other reasons.

Everyone should be familiar with the Second Amendment which guarantees our right to bear arms. There are many laws and conditions that legislatures and the courts have placed on this right. The right to purchase a gun is restricted in certain instances. The right to carry a concealed weapon is similarly restricted. Everywhere you go, there are limitations on this right.

Businesses, schools, governmental offices, and the airport, all have prohibitions on the possession of 'arms'.

Considering our country's history and development, the right to bear arms has always been crucial. As a young country, the new settlers used arms to hunt and defend themselves and their families. There was no standing army for the country, meaning citizens were called to serve in the militia of the state or country. The frontier was rural and agricultural, inhabitants were spread out and had to have their own weapons to carry if called upon. As the country grew and the frontier expanded west, there was no organized government in the territories, resulting in vast lawless areas. Having arms to provide for and defend themselves was necessary.

The Eighth Amendment provides protections from the establishment of excessive bail and fines as well as prohibitions against cruel and unusual punishments. The regulation of bail is intended to permit persons accused of a crime to be able to participate in their defense. Posting of a monetary bail allows a person to make a promise to appear for future court dates without keeping the person in a jail setting. When a person is arrested, they are brought before a judge in court within a specified period for an initial appearance or hearing, usually within 48 hours. During the hearing, the person is notified of the charges they are being accused of violating and a bail amount is set. If the person posts bail, they are released from jail under conditions while they await future court hearings and trial. The prohibition against excessive fines and cruel and unusual punishments means that penalties, be they monetary or restrictive in nature, be commensurate with the offense committed. Fines and possible imprisonment for offenses are published and determined by the legislative body enacting the law. In most instances, offenses are categorized in classifications of severity and the possible punishments are based upon those classifications. As it is commonly asked, does the punishment fit the crime?

The Fourth, Fifth and Sixth Amendments are especially important in law enforcement activities and successful trial prosecutions. What J. Edgar Hoover did for law enforcement organization and professionalism, the Warren Court did for preserving the rights of the accused and setting standards for legal investigative techniques. Chief Justice Earl Warren led the United States Supreme Court from 1953 to 1969. During this time, the nation was exiting the United Nations-led Korean Conflict and became engulfed in the Vietnam War. The nation was undergoing cultural change as it dealt with the civil rights movement and the anti-war culture. Major cultural changes were occurring, and law enforcement was caught up in the waves of change. The Warren Court ruled on several cases beginning in 1961 that continue to control how law enforcement arrests, searches, and investigations are conducted. These Fourth, Fifth, and Sixth Amendment cases set the standards for law enforcement and criminal prosecution to this day. We'll explore them in chronological order.

To set the stage, in 1914, the Supreme Court ruled in Weeks v. United States that evidence obtained without a warrant by a federal agent was not permitted at trial, thereby creating the Exclusionary Rule. The application of this doctrine meant that illegally obtained evidence could not be used by the government against a person at trial in federal court.

In 1961, the Warren Court heard arguments in the case of Mapp v. Ohio 367 U.S. 643 (1961). The issue at question in this matter was the Fourth Amendment right to be secure in a person's property. Simply put, it was a question involving search and seizure and what constituted a legal search and seizure for evidentiary use at trial. In Mapp, the Supreme Court determined that the Exclusionary Rule applies at the state as well as at the federal court level. The defendant, Ms. Dollree Mapp, was convicted of possession of pornographic materials which were found by police in her home. The police didn't have a warrant to search her home as required under the Fourth Amendment protections against warrantless searches. Ms. Mapp challenged her conviction, and the Supreme Court reversed the conviction throwing out the evidence as inadmissible, based upon the application of the Exclusionary Rule to this state case. This case changed how searches are conducted in law enforcement investigations everywhere. There are exceptions to the warrant requirement of course, but law enforcement must clearly articulate the need for the warrantless search. There is always the chance that evidence may be excluded at trial if it is not discovered under a warrant.

In 1963, the Supreme Court ruled in Gideon v. Wainwright 372 U.S. 335 (1963) that a defendant in state court is entitled to representation by counsel at trial as they would be in federal court. This was another application of the Fourteenth Amendment Due Process Clause applying federal standards to state courts.

In 1964, the Warren Court heard the case of Escobedo v. Illinois 378 U.S. 478 (1964) which concerned a Sixth Amendment issue of right to counsel. In Escobedo, the defendant Danny Escobedo was charged with the homicide of his brother-in-law. When Escobedo was arrested and detained in a police vehicle, officers attempted to question him concerning the incident. Escobedo politely responded he would like to have an attorney present during questioning. Upon arrival at the station, Escobedo was moved to the homicide unit and detectives began questioning him. Escobedo's attorney had arrived at about the same time, identified himself as Escobedo's attorney, and requested repeatedly to see his client. Officers and detectives did not permit Escobedo or his counsel to meet, indicating that questioning was continuing, even though they briefly saw each other through an open door, which was quickly shut by detectives.

Escobedo, who spoke Spanish, was addressed by a Spanish-speaking officer who allegedly made assurances that if Escobedo made statements against a co-defendant he would be permitted to 'go home'. The officer also stated that the co-defendant had indicated that Escobedo had 'pulled the trigger' in the shooting. At one point, officers put Escobedo and the co-defendant in the same room and the two subjects argued over the incident, Escobedo denying he shot the victim and accusing the co-defendant directly. During this interaction, damaging statements were made by Escobedo which indicated he had knowledge of the incident. After this exchange, a prosecuting attorney entered the interview room to take a statement from Mr. Escobedo using carefully worded questions intended to support the admissibility of evidence in court. At no point did officers or the prosecuting attorney advise Mr. Escobedo of his Constitutional rights even though he had made repeated requests to consult his attorney. Ultimately, Mr. Escobedo was convicted of murder based on the statements taken during the interrogation and statement. In February of 1963, the Illinois Supreme Court overturned the conviction ruling the statements inadmissible and the United States Supreme Court affirmed that decision in April of 1964.

The next critical case is one almost everyone is familiar with from television programs and the movies, Miranda v. Arizona 384 U.S. 436 (1966). Actually, the Warren court addressed four similar cases at the same time which presented the same Constitutional question, the right to counsel, and the right to remain silent based upon the Fifth Amendment. Miranda just happens to be the first case listed so that is the case that we all recognize and address as your 'Miranda Rights'.

The question under the Fifth Amendment was the right to have counsel present during questioning and protection from self-incrimination. In Miranda, as in the other associated cases, the defendants had been arrested and were suspected of committing various offenses, from theft to rape and homicide. During detention following their arrests, the defendants under interrogation ultimately admitted to committing the acts and signed confessions. In some cases, the detentions were hours long, in others the detention lasted several days. In all of the cases, the defendants were not advised of their Constitutional right of protection from self-incrimination and right to counsel. The defendants were all convicted at trial of the offenses charged based upon the admission of the signed confessions obtained under interrogation.

The Supreme Court ruled the confessions were inadmissible, as the defendant's right to be protected from self-incrimination based upon the Fifth Amendment had been violated. The Miranda Warnings, based upon the Court's writings are a standard law enforcement procedure used anytime a person is considered as a suspect in a crime and that person is arrested for the crime. Not all police detentions are arrests or custodial detentions that rise to the level of necessitating the 'Mirandizing' a person. However, if an officer feels that while speaking with a person during an investigative stop, issues may be raised to a level of suspicion that the person has committed a crime, the officer should halt questioning and issue Miranda Warnings to that suspect. This is a judgment call on the officer doing the investigative questioning when Miranda is required to be issued and documented.

There are various wordings of Miranda Warnings that remove gender references and such but here is what the Supreme Court wrote:

…the defendant 'must be warned prior to any questioning that he has a right to remain silent, that anything he says can be used against him in a court of law, that he has the right to the presence of an attorney, and that if he cannot afford an attorney, one will be appointed for him prior to any questioning if he so desires'.

In all four cases, the Supreme Court overturned the convictions and determined the confessions were inadmissible. Side note: although the Supreme Court overturned Miranda's initial conviction, the State of Arizona retried him on kidnapping and rape charges without introducing the confession into evidence at trial. He was convicted and sentenced to 20–30 years in prison just as he was initially sentenced.

Another common law enforcement procedure that the Warren Court determined is referred to as a 'Terry' pat down, or 'the Stop and Frisk' doctrine. In Terry v. Ohio 392 U.S. 1 (1968), the defendant had been convicted of possessing a concealed firearm following an interaction with a police detective on the streets of Cleveland. The detective was working in a shopping district where shoplifting and pickpocketing had been occurring. The detective was monitoring people on the streets and was looking for suspicious acts and behaviors. The detective indicated he was familiar with the area as he had lived and worked in that neighborhood for some 30 years. He noticed three men, one being Terry, who he didn't recognize as from the area, and who were acting in a manner that raised his suspicion that they were considering a 'stick up' at a local business. The detective believed that if this were their intentions, they may be armed with weapons to commit the act.

After monitoring their actions for some time and becoming more convinced of their intent to rob a particular business, he approached the three men on the street and engaged in a brief investigative encounter with them. He identified himself as an officer and asked the men their names. When the men responded with mumbled responses, the detective grabbed Terry, placed Terry between himself and the other men, spun him around to face the other two men, and quickly patted down the outer garments of Terry for possible weapons. Feeling a pistol in Terry's coat pocket, he ordered all three men into a nearby store, made them face the wall, removed the pistol from Terry, and then patted down the outside clothing of the other two men. Finding another pistol in one of the other men's jacket pockets, he directed the store clerk to call for police transport to the station. Both Terry and the other man were charged with carrying concealed weapons. The men were both convicted for the offenses and Terry appealed the conviction claiming his Fourth Amendment right to be protected from unreasonable search and seizure had been violated.

The Supreme Court held that a police officer may stop a suspect on the street and frisk him or her without probable cause to arrest if the police officer has a reasonable suspicion that the person has committed, is committing, or is about to commit a crime and has a reasonable belief that the person 'may be armed and presently dangerous'.

The Court in this decision pondered the varying interactions of police and citizens that occur daily. They recognized that interactions that begin peaceably, can and sometimes do turn violent or dangerous. Officers conduct frequent interactions with citizens that are not custodial detentions but range from friendly encounters to brief investigative detentions, to gather needed information from victims, witnesses, and others. The Court wrestled with balancing the protections of the Fourth Amendment of the citizen against the charge of the police and the government, to maintain peace and prevent criminal activity as well as the individual officer's right to life, liberty, and personal safety. When does the officer have the duty and the legal authority to cause a warrantless 'arrest' and 'search' of a citizen to happen? The Court ruled that given specific and articulable facts, an officer possesses at the time of the encounter, that would allow a reasonable and prudent person to believe that their, or another's safety, maybe in danger, the brief and temporary detention and search was permissible under the Fourth Amendment. The Court was very careful to limit the scope of the detention and search based upon specific, articulable facts presented by the officer to justify the 'stop and frisk'.

The Court also noted that this decision could result in a significant misuse of power by law enforcement. The warrantless 'stop and frisk' could be a significant intrusion upon a citizen resulting in embarrassment, indignity, and an intrusion of a person's cherished personal security. The Court noted that this power needed to be closely monitored and practiced with the utmost care, as it could be easily abused. The Terry decision was the last major case that the Warren Court issued which set law enforcement standards that are still being utilized today.

In 1989, the United States Supreme Court under Chief Justice William Rehnquist heard the case of Graham v. Connor 490 U.S. 386 (1989). This case involved a civil claim for damages by Mr. Graham against Connor, a police officer, and other officers of the City of Charlotte, North Carolina. Mr. Graham claimed he suffered multiple injuries when he was subject to the use of excessive force during an investigative stop by police and he filed suit for damages. The facts of this case are Mr. Graham, a diabetic, was experiencing a medical situation related to his condition. He asked a friend to drive him to a store to buy orange juice to treat the condition.

At the store, Graham entered but noticed a line at the register and concerned about the delay, quickly ran out and got back into the car directing the driver to go to a friend's home. A police officer, Connor, witnessed this activity and thought it was suspicious. He initiated an investigative stop on the vehicle and when the vehicle stopped, approached the driver to investigate.

When Connor returned to his patrol car, Graham jumped out of the vehicle, ran around it twice, then abruptly sat down on the curb and appeared to pass out. Officer Connor requested backup to the scene of the stop because of the odd behavior. After other officers arrived, Connor contacted the store to determine what if anything, had occurred. While Connor was investigating, other officers rolled Graham over and handcuffed him. Graham's driver protested saying that Graham needed sugar for his diabetes. Those officers replied that in their experience, Graham was drunk, not having a diabetic episode. Graham was treated roughly while detained, eventually being thrown into a police vehicle headfirst. An officer denied Graham orange juice while he was in the patrol car when another friend indicated that Graham needed the sugar intake to reverse the diabetic episode. Shortly thereafter, Connor learned that nothing illegal had happened at the store and officers drove Graham to his home and released him.

The Court examined this case to determine when law enforcement uses force on a person to affect an arrest or detention and what level of force is permissible under the Fourth Amendment. There is no set definition or description of permissible 'use of force' in the Fourth Amendment. Use of force is described in terms using a 'reasonableness' test. This test relies upon determining whether an officer's conduct is 'objectively reasonable' and must be based 'in light of the facts and circumstance confronting them (the officer), without regard to their underlying intent or motivation. The 'reasonableness' of a particular use of force must be judged from the perspective of a reasonable officer on the scene, and its calculus must embody an allowance for the fact that police officers are often forced to make split-second decisions about the amount of force necessary in a particular situation'.

In Graham, the Court provided guidance on when an officer uses force that use of force is reviewed under the following factors as to whether the use of force was 'reasonable'.

- Whether the totality of the circumstances justifies that use of force;
- The severity of the crime in question;
- The danger posed by the suspect to the officer or public;
- Whether the suspect is actively resisting arrest or attempting to evade arrest by flight;

- From the perspective of a reasonable officer on the scene, rather than with the 20/20 vision of hindsight;
- Allowing for the fact that officers are forced to make split-second decisions in circumstances that are often tense, uncertain, and rapidly evolving; and
- The reasonableness of the use of force is not a mechanical calculation or precise definition.

Use of force is taught to law enforcement officers within the United States by the introduction of the 'Graham factors'. Officers are taught that the use of force is an everchanging set of conditions that must be constantly re-analyzed and adjusted during an encounter with a suspect. The most docile and pleasant conversation can turn into a deadly violent encounter within seconds, and vice-versa. An officer must always adjust to the situation, applying the necessary force to maintain control over a situation while also considering the reduction of force used to maintain that control. The law enforcement officer must adjust as the subject adjusts, or the conditions change. The Graham decision is used by courts, police administrators, public review boards, and other entities when reviewing complaints of excessive use of force against law enforcement officers.

Over the last several pages, we have reviewed Constitutional law and case law precedent determined by the United States Supreme Court which law enforcement utilizes in the course of its duties. Statutory law, as the name implies, is that law that is codified in statutes and ordinances enacted by legislative bodies within the United States. This form of law is subject to change and modification by the elected representatives of the people. This form of law is derived from European common law and Judeo-Christian moral values, as well as other societal norms. The laws against murder, theft, and bearing false witness all derive from moral values.

Other laws serve to regulate the communities and maintain safety, peace, and stability within society. As an example of the changing nature of statutory law, we need only look at the recent legalization of some hallucinogenic substances. Many states have legalized the possession, use, and growing of marijuana and its derivative products. Under federal statutes, the substances remain controlled and prohibited. Besides the obvious difficulties caused by the differing interpretations, there are other issues that arise with this divide.

Laws that regulate banking and business, occupational safety, operation of commercial vehicles, professional licensing, and many more are at odds with each other. Over time, these issues will either be addressed by legislatures, or the courts will be presented with cases that challenge the long-held status quo. Eventually, society and culture will determine which way these issues will be resolved.

Chapter 5
Before September 11, 2001

To know where we are going as a society and culture, we need to understand where we have come from and what events and conditions occurred to develop the society and culture. When we discussed the history of law enforcement, we acknowledged both the influence of England and the Caribbean on the slave trade. A truly informed decision and review cannot be performed unless all the influences that led to that decision are known. Also, without context, the conditions and events that influenced those decisions lack definition, physically, emotionally, and psychologically.

On 11 September 2001, the world changed. Law enforcement, as a profession, would be changed as well. The governments of the western world would begin to concentrate efforts to try to detect, fight, and defeat terrorism. Different approaches would be utilized, but governments would make changes in laws, tactics, manpower, equipment, and technology to face the new threat. Truth is, terrorism had existed before, it just wasn't the priority for governmental use of law enforcement. Before, terrorism was an issue for the military and intelligence services, but going forward, law enforcement would be on the front lines of the fight. The military and intelligence services would still be important, as would their equipment and tactics. But this shift in priorities would usher in dramatic and sudden change which law enforcement was ill-prepared for.

In the decade leading into the new millennium, the United States was enjoying a very prosperous and energetic economic boom. The administrations of President Reagan (1981–1989), George H. W. Bush (1989–1993), and Clinton (1993–2001) had ushered in economic programs which encouraged business investment and innovation resulting in economic growth. The Cold War with the Soviet Union had ended with the collapse of the Berlin Wall and

Europe was experiencing a revival of economic health as well. It took almost 25 years for Europe to rebuild following World War II. Similarly, Japan, China, and the Eastern Pacific Nations had to be rebuilt. An estimated 60 million people had been killed in the war, military and civilian. Millions more were displaced, orphaned, or held as prisoners of war. Some regions were almost completely de-populated during the war and industrial capabilities had to be rebuilt.

Parts of eastern Europe fell under the 'Iron Curtain' of the Soviet Union, closing them off from the rest of the world. The rebuilt and modernized industry of Japan and other Far East countries led to greater availability of electronic devices and cheaper goods. Economic and political systems were changed, and those changes had a positive impact on their societies. In the mid-1980s European nations, formerly enemies, were coordinating economic interests and working toward a European community for trade. This led to the European Union which introduced the common currency of Europe, the Euro (€), on 1 January 1999. With Europe and the Far East's recovery, the United States also experienced an economic revival and technological advances.

Economic health, new ideas about government, and improving lifestyles led to an opportunity to introduce changes in society as well. In the United States, social changes concerning equal rights for minorities in employment were promoted. Affirmative action led to increases in the representation of minorities in business and government, including law enforcement. Improving economic and employment led to reductions in violent crime in large cities in the United States. Populations of the large cities grew, and law enforcement departments grew with the cities. Large cities increased their number of female, Black, and Hispanic officers as well as officers of other races. Police officers increased their education level with the number of officers having some college education growing from 19% to 37%. Departments reintroduced community policing programs, using fewer vehicle patrols and more public-friendly patrol methods such as bicycles and horses. Departments introduced more technology and special units such as anti-domestic violence, drug resistance education in schools, and victim-witness support services. According to reports from the Uniform Crime Reporting Program maintained by the FBI, the number of full-time law enforcement officers in the United States grew from 779,914 in 1992 to 1,003,441 in 2001. Economically, things were good in the United States, but as always there were problems that persisted.

Regional conflicts continued in many parts of the world, including Africa, Asia, South America, the Middle East, and Southeastern Europe. Terrorist attacks happened in many places around the globe during the 1990s perpetrated by many different groups for many differing reasons. Attacks by shooting, bombings, kidnappings, and assassinations were conducted by different separatist or cartel groups on almost every continent. In December 1992, Islamist extremists identifying themselves as Al-Qaeda bombed a hotel in Aden, Yemen targeting American soldiers. This attack marks the first reference to the now well-recognized extremist group.

On 26 February 1993, Islamic extremists detonated a truck bomb in the parking garage under the World Trade Center intending to bring the building down. Six people were killed in the bombing and over 1,000 were injured, but the buildings still stood. The main conspirator, identified as Ramzi Yousef, entered the United States on an Iraqi passport under a false name and claimed political asylum gaining entry to the country pending a hearing. Yousef was a nephew of Khalid Sheikh Muhammed, who is credited with the planning and financing of many terror attacks against the United States, including 11 September. Yousef fled to Pakistan on the day of the first Twin Towers attack and evaded arrest. In December 1994, he planted a bomb on a Philippine Airlines flight which killed one person but failed to bring down the aircraft. This attack was a trial run for Project Bojinka, translated as 'loud explosion' in Serbo-Croatian.

Project Bojinka was a plan to plant liquid-nitrogen-based explosives, mixed while in flight to defeat airport security checks, on 11 flights from the Philippines to the United States and have them detonate over the Pacific Ocean. The plan was thwarted when a fire caused by chemicals occurred in a Manila apartment Yousef was using causing the occupants to flee. A co-conspirator was arrested when he attempted to return to the apartment and retrieve a laptop containing information detailing the plan. Project Bojinka is considered the inspiration for the 11 September hijackings and suicide attacks in New York, Washington, D.C., and the crash in Shanksville, Pennsylvania. In 1995, Yousef was arrested in Pakistan and he was convicted in 1997 for the 1993 World Trade Center bombing.

On 19 April 1995, America suffered its most deadly terrorist attack on American soil to date when the Alfred P. Murrah Federal Building in Oklahoma City, Oklahoma was attacked by a truck bomb parked in front of the building. The truck bomb exploded causing a major portion of the building front to collapse resulting in 168 deaths and 680 persons injured. Timothy McVeigh was convicted of planning and conducting the attack. McVeigh was sentenced to death in federal court for the attack. McVeigh was executed in 2001, becoming the first federal prisoner since 1963 to be executed. A co-conspirator, Terry Nichols, was convicted of conspiracy and eight counts of involuntary manslaughter and received a sentence of life in prison. McVeigh and Nichols, both army veterans, identified themselves as part of the broad-based patriot movement of militias and anti-U.S. government groups. McVeigh claimed the attack was in response to the Waco, Texas assault on the Branch Davidian compound by the FBI which had occurred on the same date two years earlier.

In February of 1993, agents of the U.S. Bureau of Alcohol, Tobacco, and Firearms (ATF) attempted to enter the facility to investigate claims that the group was operating an unlicensed gun dealership. Although the ATF had obtained a warrant to enter, they decided to attempt an unannounced breach which failed resulting in four agents being killed. Investigations into the failed operation revealed the Branch Davidians had been tipped off to the planned raid by persons outside the facility. Following the ATF attempted raid, a stand-off ensued between the group and the FBI which lasted for 51 days. The FBI assumed control of the situation following the deaths of the ATF Agents as the FBI had jurisdiction over cases of criminal assaults or deaths of federal agents. Ultimately, the FBI attempted an assault which resulted in the facility catching fire, whether accidentally or started by the group leader and his members. The entire complex was destroyed, and about 80 members of the Branch Davidian group died in the fires, by suicide, or were crushed when the buildings collapsed. Timothy McVeigh had been present during the stand-off showing his support for the Davidians against the government agents, selling bumper stickers and distributing anti-government materials.

A major terrorist attack had occurred on United States soil. There had been other terror incidents targeted at an individual or a specific location or event, but nothing this significant. This incident focused the attention of law enforcement on extreme domestic right-wing groups and the so-called 'patriot movement'. The change of priorities affected primarily the FBI and other federal law enforcement agencies. Local police, except for a few large cities, did not have terrorism units or technology to investigate or counter these threats and wouldn't see major changes. Yet.

In July of 1996, another domestic terror incident occurred in Atlanta, Georgia, during the summer Olympics. Pipe bombs detonated in Centennial Olympic Park, killing one person and injuring 111 others. The bombs had been concealed under a broadcast tower in a backpack-type package. A caller had made a bomb threat indicating a bomb would go off in the area, alerting officials before the explosion. A security guard, Richard Jewel, found the suspicious package and reported the location. A bomb squad was dispatched to the area and officials started evacuating persons from the evening concert venue. The bombs detonated several minutes into the evacuation before bomb squad units could arrive to secure the devices. During the ensuing investigation, Jewel was identified as a person of interest after a report against him by a former employer to the FBI. This resulted in a search of his home, an intense investigation by authorities of him and his background, and a media siege of his home. He was never arrested and was ultimately exonerated.

In 1997, Eric Rudolph was identified as a suspect in planting the bombs in Centennial Olympic Park. He was identified after a series of three additional bombs had been detonated which matched the design of the Olympic Park bomb. One of those devices had killed a police officer and a medical worker at an abortion clinic in Atlanta. The investigation into those devices led to Rudolph as the person responsible for those devices. Rudolph fled to the wilderness and was eventually arrested in 2003 after five years on the run. The officer who arrested Rudolph noticed him behind a business at 4:00 am and thought a burglary was in progress. Rudolph's stated reasons for the bombings were to embarrass the Washington government for sponsoring abortion on demand and to cause economic harm related to the Olympic events.

After the Olympic Park bombings, there were no additional major terror attacks in the United States. Several minor ones occurred, those attacks were perpetrated by individuals described as lone wolves or by racially motivated groups such as the Aryan Nation, a White Supremacist group. Federal law enforcement agencies had started anti-terror units and new investigative techniques were developing with technology. Terrorism against the United States continued, but it occurred outside the continental borders. In 1998, the

United States Embassies in Nairobi, Kenya, and Dar es Salaam, Tanzania were destroyed in coordinated bombings. The simultaneous attacks cost the lives of 224 people and over 4,000 were injured. In October of 2000, the USS Cole, a Navy destroyer, was attacked by suicide bombers in a small boat while in the harbor at Aden, Yemen. The explosion killed 17 U.S. sailors and caused significant damage to the warship.

In the United States, local law enforcement continued to perform its' routine patrol and investigative functions. It was the federal law enforcement agencies that were adapting to the threat posed by terror groups. Of course, some large cities like New York, Los Angeles, and Washington, D.C. were also adapting in consultation with federal agencies because of their vulnerability and high target values. That would all change after 11 September 2001.

Chapter 6
After September 11, 2001

On 11 September 2001, hijackers associated with a group known as Al-Qaeda took control of four airplanes leaving from East Coast cities and traveling to West Coast destinations. Two planes departed from Boston, one from Washington Dulles, and one from Newark, New Jersey. The hijackers specifically chose these flights to coordinate take-off times, fuel loads, and low passenger occupancy. The hijackers had spent months researching and planning this morning, some even obtaining pilot licenses. The hijackers sat in the first-class section of the cabin and at a pre-planned time, assaulted the cabin crews with concealed box cutters and killed or incapacitated the flight crews taking over the flight controls. The hijackers, in teams of five men, two to fly and three to control the passengers, turned the planes around and announced to the passengers that they had a bomb on board and would destroy the plane if forced to. The instruction that they were returning to the airport and the threat of a bomb were intended to keep the passengers from fighting back. The reality was that the planes were the bombs, and the intention was not to return to the airport, but to crash the planes into significant symbols of power and economic strength.

Within an hour, three of the flights had crashed into the Twin Towers in New York City and into the Pentagon in Washington, D.C. The fourth flight crashed into a field in Shanksville, Pennsylvania when the passengers attempted to retake the plane from the hijackers in a planned counterattack. This act is sometimes referred to as the first counterattack against terrorism in the 'War on Terror'.

The attack, directed by Osama bin Ladin, the leader of Al-Qaeda, and Khalid Sheikh Muhammed, the operational director of Al-Qaeda, and uncle of Ramzi Yousef, was derived from the 'Project Bojinka' plan which had failed

Yousef in 1994. Osama bin Ladin had risen to prominence during the Afghani war against Russian occupation. He had led fighters and gained experience and notoriety among the then Central Intelligence Agency (CIA) funded and supplied Mujahedeen. Following the Russian withdrawal, bin Ladin, who had kept a roster of the men he had led, organized Al-Qaeda, translated as 'the Base', to keep fighting against what he perceived as encroachments upon the Muslim faith, homeland, and heritage.

To bin Ladin, the September 11 attacks would convince the American government to withdraw from the Middle East and withdraw their support to Israel. Bin Laden saw America as weak and vulnerable after it had withdrawn from Somalia in 1993 when 18 Army Rangers were killed in a failed raid to capture a Somali Warlord, from Lebanon in 1983 following a terror attack against a Marine barracks which had killed 241 servicemen, and its military defeat and withdrawal from Vietnam in the 1970s. Bin Ladin considered the United States (U.S.) as only a paper tiger, not able to withstand prolonged wars politically and socioeconomically. In total, 2,974 lives were lost in the 11 September attacks, not including the 19 hijackers.

In New York at the Twin Towers site, almost 400 law enforcement officers and firefighters were killed when they responded to the crash sites, most of them being trapped when the buildings collapsed. When you see video footage of the aftermath, listen closely and you can hear a high-pitched whistle or beep in the background. Those sounds are the oxygen tanks that the firefighters were wearing at the time of the collapse. The sound is to alert them that the tanks are running low on air. Unfortunately, the casualties continue to mount as responders, both public servants, military personnel, and private citizens suffer from 'WTC Syndrome' associated ailments. These persons were engaged in rescue and recovery efforts and debris removal for months following the attacks. It also includes survivors and inhabitants from the buildings and surrounding areas who were exposed to the toxic smoke, dust, and debris on surfaces. Their ailments are attributed to the debris, dust, and other contaminants they were exposed to during those post-attack moments and recovery efforts.

The Government Accountability Office (GAO) released a report in 2004 that states some 250,000 to 400,000 people were immediately exposed to toxins in New York City after the event. This includes responders, building personnel, and citizens of every age who were present in any capacity that day.

According to a report published by The Mesothelioma Center, 4,343 responders and survivors had died from health-related issues caused by the toxic dust and debris as of December 2021. This number increases each year as more succumb to their illnesses.

Following the attacks, President George W. Bush (2001–2009) formed and ordered the '9/11 Commission' to report back to the government and provide a full account of the circumstances surrounding the terrorist attacks. The commission's mandate included a review of the planning leading up to the attacks, the persons involved, and the preparedness for and immediate response to the attacks. They were also charged with providing recommendations for guarding against future attacks. This report will form the basis for law enforcement going forward in response to terrorist threats. It will also lead to major changes in how government agencies and federal law enforcement are organized as well as how the United States interacts with foreign governments to fight terrorism.

In the hours and days following the attacks, a lot of things would change. On September 11, then-Attorney General (A.G.) John Ashcroft ordered the Immigration and Naturalization Service (INS) in cooperation with the FBI to find and arrest 'Special Interest Aliens' who were known to have immigration violations in the United States. Eventually, 768 so-called 'Special Interest Aliens' were apprehended. A.G. Ashcroft ordered all special interest alien detention hearings closed to the public, family members, and the press. He further ordered United States Attorneys to seek denial of bond in all cases until cleared by the FBI of 'terrorist' connections and he ordered the identity of those persons arrested and being held kept secret. This was all done in an effort of 'risk minimization' to find out who had committed the acts on 9/11 and to thwart future attacks. Because of the limitations of governmental information sharing and no centralized way to collect information from foreign governments or other United States-based law enforcement entities regarding these persons, the average detention time was over 80 days. Of those 768 detained, 531 were deported from the United States and 8 were remanded into U.S. Marshals Service custody on their charges. The remainder were either released, had their cases dropped, or were granted some immigration status. Viewed in the light of hindsight, the right to due process under the Fourteenth Amendment of these persons was severely violated.

About a week after the attacks, A.G. Ashcroft and the Bush Administration developed guidance intended to remove 'the wall' on information sharing between the intelligence and law enforcement services. Ashcroft's intention was to ensure that every conceivable action, within the limits of the Constitution, was taken to identify potential terrorists and deter future attacks. This guidance would be presented to Congress as the 'Uniting and Strengthening America by Providing Appropriate Tools Required to Intercept and Obstruct Terrorism' Act of 2021 (hereinafter known as the USAPATRIOT Act). This law, considered and overwhelmingly passed by the House on 23 October 2001, and by the Senate on 25 October 2001, was signed into law by President Bush on 26 October 2001. This law extended the then available investigative tools and techniques used to combat organized crime and drug trafficking organizations and made them available to use against terrorism networks. Beyond greatly expanding the use of electronic means to intercept and gather information, the act also authorized numerous means of combating money laundering and terrorism financing. The law granted broad authority to the government to gather and review financial records and regulate banking institutions, both domestically and foreign. It authorized expanded authority and use of The Foreign Intelligence Surveillance Act of 1978 (FISA Act) to grant investigative warrants in secret.

The Act authorized the Attorney General and the Secretary of State to issue and pay 'rewards' to combat terrorism. Other components of the USAPATRIOT Act involved modifications of U.S. Immigration laws concerning visa applications, authorized the tripling of current personnel levels for both the Immigration and Naturalization Service (INS) and United States Customs Service (Customs), and permitted access by the Department of State and the INS to Criminal History records of persons applying for or seeking entry to the United States. The Act authorized mandatory detention of persons suspected of being involved in terrorism activities with the limited right to 'Habeas Corpus' review and proceedings in federal Circuit Courts, or the United States Supreme and Court of Appeals regarding the continued detention of that person.

The 9/11 Commission Report issued five key recommendations to the government to reorganize the government in efforts to combat terrorism and threats in a new world environment. The Commission indicated the current structure of government was born of World War II and no longer served the country adequately. The commission issued these five recommendations to address deficiencies:

- Unifying strategic intelligence and operational planning against Islamist terrorists across the foreign-domestic divide with a National Counterterrorism Center (NCTC);
- Unifying the intelligence communities under a single National Intelligence Director;
- Unifying the many participants in the counterterrorism effort and their knowledge in a network-based information-sharing system that transcends traditional governmental boundaries;
- Unifying and strengthening congressional oversight to improve quality and accountability; and
- Strengthening the FBI and homeland defenders.

The commission found that the United States had no organized governmental entity that had the responsibility for assessing vulnerabilities, protecting the homeland, and preparing for possible attacks. On 20 September 2001, President Bush appointed then Pennsylvania Governor Tom Ridge to a newly created White House position, the Homeland Security Advisor. Ridge's task would be to coordinate the resumption of services by all the different government agencies that were suspended following the attacks. Ridge would lead the Homeland Security Council in these efforts. This Council would also begin the process of determining what agencies would benefit counterterrorism efforts by being included in a proposed new departmental organization structure.

In March of 2003, with the creation of The Department of Homeland Security (DHS), Tom Ridge would be named the first Secretary of Homeland Security, a cabinet position. The 9/11 Commission had recommended the formal creation of a Department of Homeland Security which would combine resources of border and transportation security with analysis of domestic vulnerabilities and other tasks. The creation of the DHS would lead to greater ability for various federal law enforcement agencies to readily share information of foreign persons seeking entry into the United States, and those U.S. citizens traveling to and from countries where terrorism was prevalent. The Homeland Security Department model would be replicated in most states, creating a better cooperative environment at the state level to facilitate information sharing at the state and local levels as well.

Al-Qaeda and other related terror groups had declared war on the United States and the country would respond militarily as well as domestically. President Bush and his administration made it clear that there would be no differentiation between terror groups and those countries that harbored and protected them. This message was primarily aimed at Afghanistan where Al-Qaeda called home, but it also included several other troublesome regions. The Middle Eastern countries of Iraq, Iran, Pakistan, Syria, Saudi Arabia (Osama bin Ladin was Saudi-born), and northern African countries such as Somalia, Libya, and Algeria. Most of the countries of interest, and their citizens, were predominantly Muslim, following Islamic teachings. Initially, the United States responded with military special operations teams in Afghanistan targeting the Taliban which supported Al-Qaeda. Within a short time, additional military operations took aim at eliminating the Taliban entirely.

Although militarily the U.S. was successful, it only drove the Taliban further into other countries and caused the splintering of the Islamic terror networks. This led to previously insignificant groups gaining strength and causing new problems to track and defend against. The war would spread, become more costly in lives and treasure, and continue.

While all the attention was on the threat of terrorism, the United States economy and population growth continued. This led to continued growth in the law enforcement profession in the United States. Because of the actions of law enforcement, firefighters, and other first responders in response to the Twin Towers attacks, first responders were celebrated at sporting events, civic events, and other public gatherings. The sacrifices of those who had lost their lives during the Twin Towers attacks and the resulting military actions against terrorism were recognized regularly.

According to Department of Justice (DOJ) numbers, the law enforcement profession reached a peak of 1,102,599 full-time personnel in 2009. Now this number varies by the database you review because even the DOJ and the FBI Uniform Crime Reporting (UCR) systems use different metrics to record this data. The data is incomplete because reporting by law enforcement agencies throughout the country is voluntary. There are some 18,000+ law enforcement agencies at all levels across the country. Generally, about 80% of the agencies report their employment and crime report statistics each year to the FBI.

Although the numbers vary by the database, they do agree that the employment number in 2009 was the highest to date. The increases in law enforcement staffing can be attributed to increases in police community-based programs as well as general population increases.

Employment numbers would begin to dip over the next several years as the country entered a serious financial recession. That recession was caused by a U.S. housing market crash which started showing signs of failure in 2006, and the resulting economic losses would take the country years to recover from. The 'Great Recession' of 2008 in the United States would take the world economies down as well. The world would only avert another 'Great Depression' of the 1930s because of government bailouts of the U.S. banking system, the U.S. auto industry, and other industries. Countries across the world would similarly bail out their industries or take over failing industries, as the United States did with the auto industry.

Although the industries would be 'saved', the economic damage was inevitable, job layoffs, home foreclosures, and major stock market losses. It would have effects on the law enforcement profession, for years to come.

Chapter 7
The 'Great Recession' of 2008

The Great Recession of 2008 was a worldwide economic event. As the United States (U.S.) stock markets and industries go, so goes most of the world. The economic calamity was the result of the deregulation of mortgage and other financial assets which had occurred years before. In fact, we must look all the way back to President Jimmy Carter and the 1977 Community Reinvestment Act (CRA), updated under President Clinton in 1995, to find some causation. Clinton's Cabinet Secretary for the Department of Housing and Urban Development (HUD) Andrew Cuomo and two private 'government-sponsored enterprises' (GSEs-Fannie Mae and Freddie Mac) bear another portion of the blame for setting the stage for the collapse.

The CRA required banks to issue mortgages to persons with low or no credit histories. The intended goal was to lift poor and disadvantaged persons out of poverty through home ownership and reduce housing discrimination. These loans were typically adjustable-rate mortgages and were termed as 'sub-prime' in the banking industry. HUD Sec. Cuomo accelerated and encouraged banks to issue these types of loans during his tenure. He essentially turned the Federal Housing Administration (FHA) into a mortgage lender and initiated programs that rewarded brokers for issuing mortgages. The government essentially guaranteed the banks that they would be insured against losses resulting from the sub-prime mortgages.

Historically, about 8% of all mortgages were rated as sub-prime; by 2006, that percentage had risen to 20% or higher in some regions. The rate of mortgage originations to investors, meaning multi-property owners, rose from 20% to 35% within this same timeframe. Approximately 90% of sub-prime mortgages had interest rates that increased after a certain number of months had passed, not tied to the Federal Prime Lending Rate set by the Federal

Reserve. The major banks and other major financial institutions packaged and sold these sub-prime mortgages, supposedly backed by good mortgages, to and among each other as unregulated investments.

It all worked while money was being printed, interest rates were steady, home values were rising, and a person could resell or refinance the house before the interest rate timer went off beginning a rapid increase in the rate. The cracks started to show when home values started falling in 2006. This resulted in a slowing of the housing sales market.

With falling values and slowing sales, the sub-prime mortgage rates reset and started increasing and owners couldn't keep pace with payments. The U.S. household debt-to-income ratio had risen significantly and would reach 127% by 2007. Households were over-extended and couldn't make payments, the fall became a death spiral in the stock market, unemployment rates, and credit markets. The Dow market index fell 777 points on 29 September 2008, the largest ever fall. By 9 March 2009, the Dow would bottom, losing 54% of its high and falling to 6,547.05, it wouldn't recover to the previous high until September 2012. Unemployment rates rose as businesses couldn't finance their operations due to bank losses and credit tightening. Nearly nine million jobs were lost, and those jobs wouldn't be recovered until May of 2014. Household income losses in the United States alone totaled $13 trillion (with a T) and wouldn't recover until the end of 2012.

As the United States fell into the Great Recession, local governments felt the impact significantly. Job losses and failing businesses resulted in lost tax revenue. Falling home prices and foreclosures resulted in falling property tax valuations and collections. The closed businesses and vacated residences led to losses of income from utility services and uncollected revenues. Unemployed persons relied upon social service programs for financial aid, food assistance, housing, and medical services. Local and municipal governments had to slash their budgets and cut services until the economy would recover.

One of the areas in which governments dramatically cut their budgets was police services. The cuts affected all areas of police services including staffing, delivery of services, technology, and organizational management.

When looking at the operating budgets of law enforcement departments, it is important to remember that personnel are only one cost of operations. Besides the officers in all levels of positions, there are civilian employees, equipment sustainment and procurement, disposable assets and equipment, and administrative expenses to consider. When looking at a department's budget, consider that 90% of the budget will go toward employee salaries and benefits, leaving only 10% of the budget for all the other expenses. Of course, as employee length of service increases, generally so do the salary and benefit expenses.

During the years leading up to the recession, most reporting departments indicated that in the three-year period prior to 2008, their budgets had remained flat or slightly increased. The increase generally matches the cost of living or consumer price index increases. In the three-year period after the beginning of the recession, three-quarters of the departments reported that their budgets had been cut by an average of 5–10% each year. They also reported that they expected the cuts to continue into 2012 and beyond at those same levels. With the budget cuts came personnel losses. Some departments had to lay off civilian staff and officers, or not fill open positions. The consensus of various reporting services is that 10,000 or more sworn police positions were cut because of budget reductions. This doesn't include the civilian staff layoffs that would accompany the budget cuts. Some city departments were decimated by budget cuts.

In 2011, Patterson, New Jersey laid off 125 police officers, 25% of their patrol staff and they demoted 30 lieutenants and sergeants to patrol duties. The violent crime rate jumped 15% the following year. In 2010, Flint, Michigan, a city of 102,000 could only staff six officers on Saturday nights. There were 66 murders that year, eclipsing the murder rate in New Orleans, St. Louis, Newark, and Baghdad, Iraq. In 2011, Camden, New Jersey cut 164 officers, almost 50% of their staff to 204, the lowest number since 1949.

Some departments used furloughs to manage their budget cuts. Officers were mandated to reduce their number of working hours. According to the reporting data, about 28,000 officers had been mandated to reduce their hours by at least 40 hours during the year, resulting in a reduction of approximately 500 sworn officer positions. Most departments reported that their governmental entity had initiated hiring freezes to manage budget costs. 74% of cities and over 40% of county departments had hiring freezes in place. One-third reported that attrition was used to offset the budget loss, not refilling vacant positions. All of these resulted in the number of officers serving communities of all sizes across the United States dropping from 215 per 100,00 persons to 184 per 100,000 persons.

Staffing levels weren't the only things that suffered because of the budget cuts, so did police services. Departments found that with their reduced numbers they had to find other ways to do things that had traditionally been done with an officer on scene. Some departments stopped responding to traffic accidents when no injuries were reported. The information was relayed telephonically, and a report was generated electronically.

Departments stopped responding to property crimes when the event had already occurred. A report would be taken and electronically submitted. Some departments urged citizens to file their own electronic reports on certain types of cases. Investigatory follow-ups of property crimes, fugitive tracking, non-felony domestics, narcotic violations, computer-based crimes, financial crimes, and traffic violations were suspended by many departments.

Further, two-thirds of departments reported that they had cut training programs for their officers because of budget cuts. More than half reported they had canceled updates to technology as a result. Over one-third discontinued specialty units such as gang units, narcotics units, or special traffic enforcement (i.e., driving under the influence (DUI) enforcement). Over one-third sought tax increases from their government entity to cover police services and about two-thirds implemented fees for services such as alarm response and report services.

With the cuts to their budgets also came reductions in their equipment. Almost two-thirds of departments reported they had to cancel vehicle upgrades, resulting in added maintenance costs combined with the increased fuel costs which further ate into their remaining budgets. Other significant cuts include technology upgrades such as computers, license plate readers, and body cams for their patrol personnel. Almost 40% of departments reported they reduced their community policing units and about a quarter discontinued their school liaison and resource officer programs.

Many departments started programs of 'civilianization' for some traditional police services. These were civilian employee programs that used non-sworn employees serving in traditionally sworn officer roles. Some departments used civilians for mainly traffic control functions such as parades, funerals, and other special events. Some departments used civilians for property and fraud investigations and some even for crime scene investigations. Whatever the civilians were doing, they were not sworn officers and received far less pay for their functions. These programs would have their own effects and drawbacks in time.

The budget cuts and resulting changes in law enforcement departments would create an environment for problems in law enforcement going forward. For those law enforcement officers who remained during the recession, their workloads significantly increased, and their training and skill development declined. Those same officers also lost the satisfaction of resolving situations or crimes as they couldn't follow up or investigate reports further. The officer's day became a series of running from call to call, issuing reports, and dealing with more stressful situations because of increased crime and worsening economic conditions. There was no time to perform proactive patrol and proactive crime prevention functions.

The loss of specialty units resulted in officers having to respond to cases that they may not have complete training and familiarity with, such as domestic violence or narcotics. The vehicles and equipment they used became increasingly outdated and less dependable due to age. Expendable supplies such as medical equipment were no longer replaced or were entirely unavailable. Job satisfaction would suffer and knowledge transfer from generation to generation would cease. By 2013, the number of full-time police personnel and sworn officers had dropped by about 10% from the 2009 highs across the nation. As government agencies are always slower than the private sector to adjust and react to economic conditions, it takes longer for governments to recover. The number of full-time law enforcement employees nationwide wouldn't return to the 2009 levels until 2020 and wouldn't surpass those levels until 2022.

Another developing profession would also create issues within the sworn law enforcement environment, private security collaboration. Some departments turned to using private security services to operate closed-circuit television (CCTV) monitoring of traffic intersections, highways, and city neighborhoods. In some areas, private security contractors performed functions on the transit systems such as subway and bus services. Although this is a cost-saving use of available technology, it can create issues for sworn officers in case management and when considering evidentiary value for trial and court use.

Some departments, faced with major budget issues were forced into consolidation and sharing of resources with neighboring departments. Although this served to reduce duplication of equipment acquisition, it does create issues of availability and reliability and which department has priority of use and responsibility for maintenance and replacement.

Reduced officer numbers may also lead to cross-jurisdictional assistance, officer to officer. Again, this becomes an issue for court resolution. Although it can be beneficial and efficient to share resources, it can also be detrimental if faced with an emergency that affects both agencies, such as a widespread natural disaster. Departments were forced into flexibility and versatility in dealing with the budget cuts and still providing their citizens with expected and obligated services.

The effects of the 'Great Recession of 2008' would be significant and long-lasting on law enforcement departments of all sizes across the country. Although modernization would be forced upon the departments with the use of computer reporting and other technological improvements, these would again increase the distance of the officer from the community. A cold computer-based report is different than a caring person who takes the time to listen and prepare the report of the citizen's complaint. The discontinuance of specialty units would lead to reduced enforcement and identity of gang members, narcotics enforcement, property crime enforcement, financial crimes, and other more investigative intense enforcement activities.

As the economy began to improve and recover, the stage would be set for the next crisis in law enforcement. Everything that had occurred would contribute in some way to the developing crisis. That crisis has caused major disruptions to our society and culture. It didn't happen overnight; it took years to develop. That crisis is marked by significant incidents that serve as milestones which we will examine going forward. Those events and their influence on society, culture, and politics, are threatening to end the profession of law enforcement as we currently recognize it. As with all change, the choice is between adaptation and extinction, we'll see what happens in the years to come.

Chapter 8
'Great Recession' Recovery

The 'Great Recession' of 2008 impacted government law enforcement in a multitude of ways. First and foremost, personnel staffing. As noted in the previous chapter, full-time and sworn officer numbers were significantly reduced, losing about 10% nationwide. Departments offset the loss of full-time sworn personnel with 'civilianization' and other means such as technology, citizen self-reporting systems, and sometimes just stopping responses to certain types of calls for service.

Equipment purchasing and maintenance were also significantly impacted as reduced budgets led to the cancelation of orders to replace vehicles, radios, computers, and other items. In the case of vehicles, the recession also resulted in significant price increases in fuel costs that also had to be offset within budgets, further reducing available funds. As we all know, the longer you drive a vehicle, the more expensive it begins to get with upkeep and maintenance. Vehicles just don't last forever and depending on the amount and type of use the vehicle gets, they wear out. Preventive maintenance being performed can extend the life some, but there are many parts that are expendable like tires, brakes, exhaust systems, etc. All those costs take a bite of out the remaining operating budget.

Then there is the effect on training programs and personnel training. Many training programs exist, but they cost money to attend and facilitate. When there is no budget for the programs, skills stagnate, and training suffers. When it comes to firearms skills, ammunition, and range time costs money, reduce the frequency, and money is saved. This also results in lower skills and less time spent 'role-playing' encounters, reducing psychological readiness for non-routine encounters. As stated earlier, law enforcement is filled with repetition and boredom, with some terror and uncertainty sprinkled in. When training and readiness diminish, complacency creeps in and then mistakes happen. Another form of training that suffered is keeping officers current with laws, tactics, and trends. For example, the rise of Mixed Martial Arts (MMA) training as a form of physical fitness led to increases in persons familiar with the techniques associated with this form of fighting. When a law enforcement officer had an encounter with a person who was familiar with this form of training, the officer was at a tactical disadvantage when it came to gaining control in a physical altercation. This could easily lead to an officer considering raising the level of force used to resolve the situation.

By 2012 and 2013, the country was emerging from the economic disaster. Private industry had regained its' strength and unemployment was easing. The government, which lags private industry, was starting to see increases in budgets as revenues improved. America's population had continued to grow throughout the recession and much of that growth had occurred in the cities and surrounding suburbs. Governments began filling the vacancies caused by budget cuts, layoffs, attrition, and hiring freezes within their law enforcement departments. As job positions opened, competition drove salary and benefit package increases for recruits. With pressure to refill positions to alleviate prolonged response times, resume services that had been suspended, and restaff specialty units, some corners may have been cut in the name of expediency. Also, some hiring standards may have been lowered to broaden the pool of candidates.

There is no national standard for law enforcement positions, each state sets its own standards and rules. Heck, the federal government has multiple federal law enforcement agencies that do specific jobs and there are no standardized hiring requirements for the federal government either. Each agency determines its own standards and then the candidates attend an agency-specific academy for training. One federal agency may require a college degree or specific work or military experience to qualify and another may be as simple as 18 years old and a clean criminal record. The Federal Law Enforcement Training Center (FLETC) based in Glynco, Georgia does provide some standardized basic training practices that are implemented across all agencies, but not the entire training program. FLETC provides a lot of advanced training courses to federal law enforcement, which depending on the program, may be open to non-federal law enforcement personnel as well.

The lack of standardization of hiring and training practices means that there is no minimum standard that a person entering law enforcement must meet to be in the profession. It doesn't take a whole lot of imagination to see where this may lead to problems within the profession. A person who may not meet the criteria set by one state may simply move to another state where now they may qualify. One state may require a two or four-year college certificate to qualify whereas a neighboring state may only require certain age and criminal history standards. There are also the economic considerations with the cost of the two or four-year college certificate being born by the candidate wanting to enter the profession.

That brings up another difference, educational programs. They are as varied as the states. Some large cities and most state agencies operate their own academies, training the candidates after hiring them into the positions. These training programs are generally well-run, updated, consistent, and professional. Some training programs are operated by professional training schools which offer the training, at a cost to the student, for profit. As with any school, you can get great variety in the quality of education. Some of these training programs hire retired law enforcement officers to teach the courses which may result in students receiving instruction in outdated techniques and philosophies. It can also introduce the student to less than currently acceptable practices, both physically, emotionally, and socially. When it comes to a two or four-year college program, these vary as well. Some college programs are geared toward law, legal theory, and philosophy whereas others are steered toward law enforcement history, structure, and sociology. J. Edgar Hoover had envisioned the professional law enforcement officer as educated at a college level. There just hasn't been any formal program developed and incorporated nationwide to fulfill that vision.

Over the period from 2013 until 2020, law enforcement employment numbers would see gradual and sustained growth. Of course, this doesn't mean all the gains were in the number of sworn officers, some of those gains would be civilians and support staff which had been lost during the recession. New positions had been created as well with the implementation of new technology and new non-sworn civilian positions to reduce officer call backlogs and responsibilities. Over this same period, law enforcement would be challenged like never before by advances in technology, the aftermath of the recession, and political pressures that once initiated, it had little chance to control.

Chapter 9
2012 and 2013

As the country emerged from the 'Great Recession', law enforcement departments were starting to rebuild their personnel, equipment, and training programs. The process would take time, years in fact, as previously stated until 2020 to recover staffing levels to prerecession numbers. Law enforcement departments would start to see gradual increases in their budgets which would permit them to modernize outdated equipment and replace equipment that had been lost to budget cuts. Some recession processes and procedures would remain in place such as non-response to certain calls and self-reporting by citizens, service fees for certain types of calls and administrative records, and civilian employees performing some functions previously performed by sworn officers.

The one thing nobody can ever be prepared for is the unexpected, and law enforcement is no exception. In this chapter, and in the following chapters, we will review several incidents and events that occurred that changed how our society and culture see law enforcement. The effects may not be immediate, as with all things, change takes time to happen.

On 26 February 2012, at approximately 7:00 pm, in the town of Sanford, Florida, one such event would occur. During the evening hours of that rainy night, 17-year-old Trayvon Benjamin Martin, a Black male, was walking to his father's fiancée's townhouse in the Retreat at Twin Lakes community on the sidewalk. He was talking on his cell phone to a friend, Rachel Jeantel, in Miami and carrying a bag of Skittles and an Arizona watermelon cooler which he had purchased at a nearby 7-Eleven. Trayvon, a young Black male, was wearing a gray hooded sweatshirt (a 'hoodie') with the hood up over his head and face and walking slowly along the sidewalk in the light rain. At this same time, George Zimmerman, an area resident, and member of the local neighborhood watch, was driving in his Sport Utility Vehicle (SUV) to Target to complete an errand. Zimmerman, a Hispanic male, noticed Martin and according to statements recorded later by police, he considered Martin's actions suspicious.

Zimmerman called the Sanford police and told the dispatcher that Martin was not a resident of the community, was walking leisurely in the rain, and was looking at houses as he walked. At 7:09 pm, Martin also called the Sanford police and reported that a suspicious person was staring at him. While Zimmerman was on the phone with the dispatcher, he noticed Martin starting to walk toward his location and he told the dispatcher the subject was 'coming to check him out'. Zimmerman asked how long it would take for police to respond and when he was told an officer was en route, he responded frustratedly, "These assholes, they always get away."

At this same time, Martin was talking with Jeantel and complained to her 'that a man was watching him' and described the man as 'a creepy-ass cracka'. Jeantel warned Martin that the man may be a rapist and advised him to run. Martin did.

Zimmerman saw Martin starting to run away and told the dispatcher, "Shit, he's running," and started back to where he had exited his car to follow Martin. The dispatcher asked Zimmerman if he was intending to chase the subject and when Zimmerman responded, "Yeah," the dispatcher told him he didn't need to do that and directed him to meet police officers by the mailboxes. Martin agreed and a few seconds later the four-minute call to the police ended.

What happened next was the subject of much debate and issue at the trial of Zimmerman. Besides Zimmerman, there were two primary witnesses who provided an account of the events that transpired next. There were also several other neighborhood witnesses who provided some corroborating information.

Zimmerman told police that while he was walking over to where his vehicle was parked, Martin jumped out from behind some bushes and confronted Zimmerman exclaiming, "What the F@%4's your problem, homey?" And when Zimmerman responded, "I don't have a problem," Martin said, "Now you have a problem," and Martin struck Zimmerman in the nose. Zimmerman was knocked to the grass by the punch and Martin continued to pummel him while he was down. Zimmerman indicated he started screaming for help and that he couldn't see and couldn't breathe.

Ms. Jeantel reported a slightly different version of events to the police. She was still on the phone when Zimmerman and Martin initially met. She said she heard Martin ask Zimmerman, "Why are you following me?" And heard a man who was breathing hard respond, "What are you doing here?" She then heard a bump, which she thought was Martin's headset falling to the ground. As she yelled, "Trayvon, Trayvon," she heard what she described as 'wet grass sounds' and then 'kind of heard', Martin say, "Get off, get off," and then the phone connection ended.

Zimmerman reported to police that the altercation that occurred between himself and Martin continued while he was down, that Martin had grabbed his head and was hitting it on the sidewalk. Zimmerman was able to get back to the grass and yell, "Help me, help me. He's killing me."

Martin, who was then atop Zimmerman, attempted to cover his mouth to silence him and said, "You're going to die tonight." Zimmerman attempted to slide away from Martin and his jacket and shirt slid up. At this point, Zimmerman said he felt Martin's hand on his side where his firearm was and that he thought Martin was trying to get his firearm. Zimmerman said Martin again attempted to bang his head on the ground and it was at this time that Zimmerman pulled the firearm and fired one shot, striking Martin in the chest and fatally wounding him. Police arrived on the scene within minutes of the shooting.

A local community resident, Mr. Good, reported to police investigators that he had witnessed part of the confrontation, that he had heard the yelling, and saw a man in a dark-colored sweatshirt atop a man in a lighter-colored sweater in a fight; that the man on top was Black and the other man lighter skin-colored. Mr. Good seeing the fight, started back to his home to call 911, and once inside, he heard a gunshot. When he went outside again, he noticed two guys with flashlights asking what was going on, and that the one guy who was on the bottom said that he had shot the other guy in self-defense.

One of the responding officers, Timothy Smith, noted in his report that after taking Zimmerman's gun and securing it, he placed Zimmerman in handcuffs. Smith noted that Zimmerman was bleeding from the nose, had blood on the back of his head and that the back of his jacket was wet and covered with grass. Zimmerman was transported to the Sanford police station where he was questioned for five hours by another officer and a detective. Martin's body was transported to the city morgue and marked as 'John Doe' as his identity was unknown at the time.

The following day, Tracy Martin, Trayvon's father filed a missing person's report regarding his son. At 9:20 am, police officers arrived at his fiancée's condo and showed him photos which he identified as his son, Trayvon. Also on this day, police investigated Zimmerman's claims subjecting him to additional questioning and a voice stress analysis test, which he passed, to verify his statements. The police escorted him to the scene where they videotaped him re-enacting the events of the previous night. On 12 March, Police Chief Bill Lee made a statement that, "until we (Sanford police) can determine probable cause to dispute Zimmerman's claim of self-defense, we have no grounds to arrest Zimmerman." Chief Lee also stated that the whole situation is very unsettling and that if Zimmerman, and Martin, could go back and do things differently that night, they probably would.

Zimmerman's claim of self-defense was rooted in Florida's 'Stand Your Ground' self-defense law, so-called 'Stand Your Ground' laws, also called 'no duty to retreat' or 'line in the sand' laws, made up the self-defense statutes in 38 states across the nation. These laws indicate that a person has the right to defend themselves in any place where they are legally present, using necessary force up to and including deadly force. This law applies when a person is attacked or perceives that a violent attack on themselves is about to occur. The legal doctrine differs from the 'Castle Doctrine' which indicates a person has a right to defend themselves within their own home, and in some jurisdictions, within their vehicle or workplace. Each state defines the self-defense law differently and of course, uses case law precedent to determine whether either doctrine applies in claims of self-defense.

But that wasn't the end of the story. Tracy Martin, Trayvon's father enlisted the aid of a Tallahassee civil rights attorney by the name of Benjamin Crump to bring a prosecution against Zimmerman. Crump turned to the media to elevate the story and put pressure on the Florida State prosecutor to charge Zimmerman. Crump scheduled press conferences with Trayvon's parents speaking about the tragic loss. He called for the release of the 911 tapes implying something was being hidden; this turned the case into a national story. He organized rallies to call for justice for Trayvon and he enlisted African American leaders such as Jesse Jackson and Al Sharpton to support the cause.

An internet-based/social media campaign started a petition to prosecute Zimmerman which gathered 2.2 million signatures asking for Zimmerman to be charged with murder. The case was penned as either about racial profiling or deriding the self-defense 'Stand Your Ground' laws. Lebron James and the Miami Heat NBA basketball team posted photos of the team wearing 'hoodies' and players wrote messages on their shoes calling for justice and reading 'RIP Trayvon Martin.' Other NBA players including Carmelo Anthony and Amare Stoudemire of the New York Knicks also posted photos of themselves in 'hoodies' with a caption that read 'I am Trayvon Martin!' The National Basketball Players Association (NBPA) called for Zimmerman's arrest, opined that Trayvon Martin was murdered, and called for investigations into the Sanford police department. The NBPA criticized the Sanford police for 'their silence in the face of injustice…and they cannot be trusted to safeguard the citizens of the Sanford community equally'. In May, President Barack Obama (2009–2017) commented that if he 'had a son, he'd look like Trayvon Martin'.

In late March, with all the national attention, Governor Rick Scott appointed a special prosecutor, State Attorney Angela Corey, to review the evidence of the case as an independent reviewer. President Obama directed U.S. Attorney General Eric Holder and the Justice Department to investigate whether Zimmerman had violated Martin's civil rights in this incident. The Sanford Police Chief was placed on paid administrative leave because of the attention and pressure on the city.

A review of the case file by the special prosecutor uncovered no new evidence to dispute the claims of Zimmerman. The FBI conducted interviews and determined there was no evidence to support civil rights violations against Zimmerman. But on 11 April, without convening a Grand Jury hearing, Angela Corey ordered Zimmerman arrested and charged with second-degree murder and lesser charges of manslaughter. Zimmerman surrendered himself the next day and on 20 April 2012, he posted bail and was released with an ankle-monitor device. His bail was revoked in early May for redetermination of financial ability of bail and in July after a new higher bail was set, he was again released once that bail was met.

Zimmerman and his attorneys also used the internet and media to get their side of the story out. Zimmerman did interviews with friendly media sources. He raised funds for his legal defense using the internet and social media. Zimmerman's attorneys presented pre-trial motions but stopped short of making a motion for pre-trial determination of immunity from prosecution as available in Florida's self-defense law as they didn't want to reveal their strategy before the actual trial began.

On 20 June 2013, the trial began. During opening statements, the prosecutor incorrectly quoted Zimmerman and gave the jury the impression that Zimmerman was prejudiced against Martin due to his race. That Zimmerman lied about his injuries sustained in the confrontation and claimed that Zimmerman was just a 'wannabe cop' on the neighborhood watch. The defense played the 911 recording between Zimmerman and the dispatcher which set the stage to dispute the prosecution's claim. During the trial, the prosecution presented witnesses who did not support the implications of racial bias, Zimmerman's lack of injuries, or anything other than what Zimmerman had claimed. One prosecution witness even testified that there had been a series of burglaries in the community in the preceding several months which prompted the neighborhood to form a watch group. The defense presented a witness who had experienced one of these break-ins, a home-invasion burglary. The defense introduced evidence that Martin had ample opportunity to leave the area, that Martin had initiated the confrontation, and that Martin had caused injury to Zimmerman which caused him to fear for his life. That Zimmerman's actions were self-defense and that according to Florida law, he should be acquitted of all charges.

More witnesses were called and for most of them, they supported Zimmerman's account of the story. When the forensic expert testified about the fatal gunshot and injuries sustained by Zimmerman as medically consistent with his version of the events, that really hurt the prosecution's case. When the prosecutor put Ms. Jeantel on the witness stand, the language she used during her testimony involved racial slurs and slang words. During one response she said that Trayvon had told her that 'the nigga is still following him'.

Referring to the 'N' word in open court testimony in such a way influenced the jury's interpretation of her credibility and testimony. On cross-examination, Ms. Jeantel was forced to admit to several lies she had told to the police during her initial questioning. This served to further neutralize her testimony and her credibility.

On 13 July 2013, after 15 hours of deliberations, Zimmerman was found 'Not Guilty' on all charges by the jury of six women, five white and one of Hispanic descent. A juror who was interviewed later by CNN's Anderson Cooper said the jury never felt that race played a part in the incident, that they had felt that although Zimmerman may have been guilty of bad judgment by getting out of his vehicle, that doesn't mean he lost the right to defend himself if attacked; that they felt Martin reacted angrily at Zimmerman's watching him and attacked Zimmerman in that anger; that this was a tragedy that shouldn't have happened, but unfortunately did.

Reaction publicly to the verdict was split, by political lines and along racial lines. President Obama simply said, "The jury has spoken," and asked for prayers for the parents who lost their son. Former President Jimmy Carter (1977–1981) commented that the jury had made the 'right decision'. Former NBA star Charles Barkley also felt the jury had reached the right decision.

The reaction was immediate and direct on social media and on the streets of America. Protests started in numerous U.S. cities calling for Justice for Trayvon. One community organizer in Oakland opened her Facebook account and made a post that included three words: 'Black lives matter'. That was the first time those words were linked together in the public square of social media. Soon after several racial justice groups were formed, including the Black Lives Matter network, Dream Defenders, and Black Youth Project 100, they merged later under an umbrella organization titled Movement for Black Lives. One year later, these groups would again have cause to call for justice for a young man whose life was taken.

On 24 February 2015, the United States Justice Department (DOJ) concluded its Civil Rights investigation into the matter and closed the case without filing any charges. In the statement released by the Department of Justice, U.S. Attorney General Eric Holder stated, 'The death of Trayvon Martin was a devastating tragedy. It shook an entire community, drew the attention of millions across the nation, and sparked a painful but necessary dialogue throughout the country...' A.G. Holder went on to issue the conclusion that the high standards set for federal hate crime prosecution cannot be met here, in this case. He continued that the country needs to take steps to ensure that future incidents like this do not occur.

The Martin case highlighted the use of social media and internet websites to generate and bring public pressure on public officials in legal cases. The wide-reaching aspect of social media postings acts to rapidly spread information across the country and the world. Social media sites are unregulated sources of information which can result in erroneous information being spread and unfortunately, influencing public opinion. The involvement of political activists, sports celebrities, media figures, and other celebrities in the social media universe results in the enhancement of public awareness of such incidents. Although it is true that social media does provide an avenue of information sharing, without confirmation and contextual meaning, the negative may outweigh the positive.

Another aspect of this case that affects how law enforcement and the criminal justice system are viewed is the charging of Zimmerman by the special prosecutor, Angela Corey, of murder charges without Grand Jury proceedings. This is a right afforded to criminal defendants in the Fifth Amendment to the Constitution. Grand Jury proceedings are meant to provide a check between the criminal justice system and the person being charged with a crime. This ensures that criminal prosecutions are not initiated without legal cause. A Grand Jury reviews the evidence gathered by investigators, presented by a prosecutor, with context as to the legal basis of a violation of criminal statutes and then determines if the evidence supports a criminal indictment. In the Zimmerman arrest and criminal charges, the special prosecutor bypassed this critical element of the criminal justice system, essentially violating George Zimmerman's Constitutional right to due process. It appeared that the criminal charges were filed to relieve the media pressure and attention surrounding this case, although Ms. Corey claimed that had no influence on her decision.

Lastly, the Martin case highlighted the nationwide use 'Stand your ground' based standards for self-defense laws that existed across the various States. The death of Martin focused light on these laws and caused state legislatures across the country to review their statutory requirements. Currently, 37 states have 'Stand your ground' based self-defense laws. Of those 37, 8 have no statutory regulation, the self-defense law is entirely based upon judicial interpretation and legal precedent within the state.

Chapter 10
July 2014

After the Trayvon Martin jury decision was announced, protests and demonstrations occurred throughout the United States. The federal civil rights case was still open, and the U.S. Department of Justice continued to investigate the matter. Racial justice organizations that had developed out of the Martin case continued to be active and call for justice. Celebrities continued to be interviewed and give opinions on matters of racial disparity, unequal treatment, and justice denied. The anger and distaste of the Martin decision may have subsided, but it hadn't been extinguished. Only one year and four days after the Zimmerman verdict was announced, another major incident would occur that would rekindle the fires of protest and demonstration. This time, the effects would be immediate.

On 17 July 2014, a 43-year-old man named Eric Garner died after New York Police Department (NYPD) Officer Daniel Pantaleo applied an unauthorized 'chokehold' to Garner while attempting to detain him for a minor violation. On that day, a plainclothes NYPD officer, Justin D'Amico, approached Garner at about 3:30 pm, on the sidewalk outside a Staten Island beauty supply business. According to witnesses, including Ramsey Orta, who recorded the interaction between Garner and the NYPD officers, Garner had recently broken up a fight on the street which may have drawn the attention of the police to Garner. Officers accused Garner of selling 'loosies' (single cigarettes without a tax stamp) in violation of New York state law, Garner had been arrested by NYPD for this offense previously on several occasions. Garner protested saying, "Get away, for what?" Garner continued, "Every time you see me you want to mess with me. It stops today. I'm tired of it." Garner then said, "Everyone here will tell you I didn't do anything; I didn't sell anything." He explained that he was minding his own business and asked the officer to just leave him alone.

At this point, another officer, Daniel Pantaleo, approached Garner from behind and attempted to handcuff him but when he touched Garner's arm, Garner pulled his arms away and exclaimed, "Don't touch me. Please." Officer Pantaleo then placed one arm around Garner's neck and upper chest and the other arm under Garner's armpit and tried to pull Garner backward to the ground. The video shows Garner and Pantaleo bouncing off a store window and then Garner goes down to his knees and forearms. Pantaleo continues to hold Garner while Garner goes to a face-down position on the sidewalk where uniformed officers move it to handcuff and secure Garner. Pantaleo holds Garner for 15 seconds while officers secure him then releases Garner's neck and uses his hands to hold Garner's face down on the sidewalk. While in this position, Garner exclaims repeatedly, "I can't breathe." He makes this statement 11 times while he lies in this prone position face down on the sidewalk. One of the officers requested an ambulance for Garner indicating the suspect was having trouble breathing but also comments that he 'did not appear to be in great distress'.

Garner lay motionless in a prone face-down position for several minutes before the ambulance arrived. Officers monitored Garner and when he lost consciousness, they repositioned him onto his side to ease his breathing. Garner lay on the sidewalk for seven minutes until the ambulance arrived and when medics arrived, they checked his pulse but did little else for two minutes before lifting him onto a stretcher. During the transport to a nearby hospital, Garner suffered a heart attack and was pronounced dead one hour later at the hospital.

On 19 July, the *New York Post* published an article, citing unnamed sources, claiming that the medical examiner had found no damage to Garner's 'windpipe or neckbones'. That afternoon, Al Sharpton organized a protest in Staten Island condemning the use of the chokehold during Garner's arrest and stated 'there is no justification' for it.

On 20 July, Officers Pantaleo and D'Amico were assigned desk duties pending investigation, officer Pantaleo was stripped of his badge and firearm. The four medics involved in the transport were suspended on 21 July pending investigations.

On 1 August, the medical examiner released the preliminary autopsy report indicating that the cause of death was a homicide. In New York, homicide is defined as death caused by the intentional actions of another person or persons, not necessarily an intentional death or a criminal death. The report indicated the cause of death was 'compression of the neck (a chokehold), compression of the chest, and prone positioning during physical restraint by police'. The medical examiner also cited contributing facts of pre-existing asthma and heart disease.

On 19 August, Staten Island District Attorney Daniel M. Donovan Jr. presented evidence in the matter to a Grand Jury against Officer Pantaleo. On 29 September, the Grand Jury began hearing the evidence and testimony in the matter. Officer Pantaleo testified before the Grand Jury on 21 November for two hours. After two months of deliberations, on 3 December 2014, the Grand Jury concluded there was insufficient evidence to indict Officer Pantaleo in the death of Eric Garner. By law, Grand Jury evidence, testimony, and charges are secret.

Between 3 and 28 December, over 50 protests and 'dies-ins' were held in protest of the Grand Jury result. Protests and 'dies-ins' were held in cities across the United States and the United Kingdom at London Westfield in a show of solidarity.

On 20 December, two NYPD officers were killed in an ambush attack in Bedford-Stuyvesant, Brooklyn. The suspected gunman, identified as Ismaaiyl Brinsley, claimed the attack was because of the death of Eric Garner and Michael Brown which had occurred on 9 August 2014, in Ferguson, Missouri. After the attack, Brinsley entered the subway and committed suicide.

Following Garner's death, the NYPD Commissioner ordered a review of all NYPD training programs concerning the use of force during detention and arrest, including restraint holds. On 8 June 2020, the State Assemblies of New York passed the Eric Garner Anti-Chokehold Act, which provides that any police officer in the State of New York who causes injury or the death of a person by use of a 'chokehold or similar restraint' will be guilty of a felony punishable up to 15 years in prison. The Act was signed into law by Governor Andrew Cuomo on 12 June 2020.

The United States Department of Justice (DOJ) opened a Civil Rights investigation into Eric Garner's death on 3 December 2014, following the Grand Jury determination of no indictment. The investigation was closed on

16 July 2019, after almost five years of exhaustive investigation. The DOJ concluded that there was 'insufficient evidence to prove beyond a reasonable doubt that the police officers who arrested Garner on Staten Island on 17 July 2014, acted in violation of the federal civil rights statute'. The DOJ report cited that the video of the incident showed that Officer Pantaleo attempted two different NYPD-trained and approved control techniques during the encounter with Garner. The report was significantly delayed due to administrative actions concerning Pantaleo and his defense of those disciplinary actions. Pantaleo was fired from the NYPD after those hearings on 19 August 2019.

The DOJ report concluded that the officers had reason to take Garner into custody as they were on a special assignment to deter the unlicensed sale of cigarettes in that area and Garner resisted a lawful arrest, both verbally and physically. Initially, Officer Pantaleo attempted an 'arm-bar' which involved pulling the hand of a person down while the officer moved to their rear to place handcuffs on the suspect; that Garner resisted this attempt by pulling away and turning his body to defeat the maneuver; that Officer Pantaleo then attempted a 'rear takedown' or 'seatbelt' technique to gain control of Garner. This maneuver involves the placing of one hand under a person's armpit and the other hand across their shoulder and chest to unbalance the person and bring them to the ground.

It was clear that Officer Pantaleo had his palm facing away from Garner's neck. This suggested that Officer Pantaleo did not intend to place Garner in a chokehold. The DOJ also noted that the size disparity between Garner, 6' 2" and nearly 400 pounds, and Officer Pantaleo, contributed to the inability of Pantaleo to secure Garner properly. During the attempt and while Pantaleo had a hold of Garner's chest, the two fell backward into a store window, buckling it and bouncing off. It was during this fall that Pantaleo's hold on Garner's chest changed, and Pantaleo's hand wrapped around Garner's neck. This condition lasted for seven seconds. The report further noted that at no time while Pantaleo applied the control hold or had his hand on Garner's neck did Garner indicate he couldn't breathe. It was only after Pantaleo had released the hold and while Garner was being handcuffed in the prone position that Garner made those statements.

Following Garner's death, the phrase 'I Can't Breathe' became a slogan for anti-police brutality and racial justice activists. Again, popular players in the NBA donned warm-up gear with the slogan prior to their games. The slogan also was displayed by players in the National Football League (NFL) as did the Georgetown University Men's and University of Notre Dame Women's NCAA college basketball teams. Musicians also picked up on the slogan and incorporated it into their art, including it as a lyric or title. President Obama and Attorney General Holder publicly applauded NBA star Lebron James for wearing the shirts with the slogan.

Chapter 11
August 2014

On 9 August 2014, less than a month after Eric Garner died following his encounter with NYPD officers, there would be another event that would engulf the nation. This time a police officer would be involved in the shooting of an unarmed Black male. The news would spread via social media almost immediately after the event. There would be no time for investigators to release information, the storyline would already be determined in the public's eyes. A police officer had shot an unarmed, young, Black male, who had his hands up above his head saying, "Don't shoot." The slogan 'Hands Up, Don't Shoot' would reverberate across the country and join 'I Can't Breathe' in the racial justice movement. Unfortunately, for many in the Ferguson, Missouri area, the results would be disastrous.

Just before noon on 9 August 2014, 18-year-old Michael Brown and a friend, 22-year-old Dorian Johnson, were walking in the middle of Canfield Drive, a street in Ferguson, Missouri after visiting the 'Ferguson Market' store. Ferguson is a community on the outskirts of St. Louis, Missouri, and has a high percentage of neighborhoods at or near the poverty level. At 11:53, that store had reported to Ferguson Police a theft of a box of Swisher cigars and that when the clerk attempted to stop the perpetrator, the subject had shoved the clerk out of the way and left on foot.

Officer Darren Wilson of the Ferguson Police Department was driving his Chevrolet Tahoe Sports Utility Vehicle (SUV) squad westbound on the same street after leaving a medical call and heard the radio report that a 'stealing in progress' was occurring at a nearby store. The report described the suspect as a Black male wearing a white t-shirt running toward the Quik Trip. A second radio announcement at 11:57 am indicated that the suspect was wearing a red St. Louis Cardinals baseball cap, wearing a white t-shirt, yellow socks, and khaki shorts. This announcement indicated the suspect was accompanied by a second male subject.

As Office Wilson drove westbound, he saw two male subjects walking in the middle of the street traveling eastbound. As he approached the subjects, he stopped and advised them to get out of the street onto the sidewalk. Johnson responded with 'were almost to our destination' and Brown replied, "F$%@ what you have to say?" According to Officer Wilson's testimony. The pair continued to walk eastbound after the exchange toward the rear of the police vehicle. Officer Wilson backed up and positioned the vehicle in front of the two male subjects to block their path. Officer Wilson started opening his squad door and instructed the subjects to 'come here'.

Brown started approaching the vehicle and said, "What the f$%@ you going to do?" and Officer Wilson closed the door in response to Brown's advance. Officer Wilson attempted to open the vehicle door again to push Brown back away from the vehicle and instructed him to 'get back'. At this time, Brown started punching Officer Wilson through the open vehicle door window. Brown landed a 'glancing' punch to the left side of Wilson's face causing Wilson to lean back in his seat and avoid further attempted punches. Officer Wilson raised his left arm to try to get Brown's arms away from his face as Brown continued to engage. Brown turned to his left and handed Johnson several packages of 'cigarillo cigars' and at this point, Officer Wilson attempted to gain control of Brown's right arm by grabbing it. Brown again punched Officer Wilson and this time, the blow 'jarred' Wilson, he testified. Officer Wilson considered using his mace or baton but couldn't reach them while engaged with Brown. Officer Wilson drew his firearm and pointed it at Brown telling him to stop or he would shoot him while ordering him to get on the ground.

According to Wilson's testimony, Brown replied, "You're too much of a f$%@ing pussy to shoot me," and grabbed Wilson's gun turning it toward Wilson's hip area. Officer Wilson used both hands to push his gun back toward Brown and pulled the trigger twice, but the weapon did not fire. Wilson pulled the trigger again and that time the weapon fired, hitting Brown's right hand/thumb area. Brown attempted to strike Wilson several additional times so Wilson fired again, missing Brown. At this time, Brown disengaged and started running eastbound away from the vehicle. Johnson also fled and reportedly hid behind a nearby vehicle. Wilson exited his vehicle and radioed for backup officers to his location then ran after the fleeing Brown yelling for him to stop and get on the ground. After a short distance, Brown stopped and turned to face Wilson, paused, and made a 'grunting noise'. Brown started running at Officer Wilson with his right hand under his shirt in his waistband. Officer Wilson repeated the commands to stop and get down on the ground and when Brown did not respond, he fired several rounds at Brown. Brown paused after these shots were fired and Wilson stopped shooting, then Brown resumed running at Officer Wilson. Wilson retreated and as he was retreating fired additional rounds, again Brown paused and then resumed his charge. Officer Wilson testified that he fired a third set of rounds when Brown was between eight and ten feet away from him and Brown fell face down after the final round was discharged. Officer Wilson testified that backup officers arrived about 20 seconds after the final round was fired. The whole incident had lasted about 90 seconds.

As additional units arrived, the scene became chaotic. Local neighborhood residents and persons on the roadway began to gather and surround the scene. Units responding to the scene requested a supervisor and additional units. At 12:07, St. Louis County Police were notified and dispatched to the scene. By 12:15, St. Louis County Police began arriving on scene. By 1:00 pm, 12 units had arrived on the scene. By 2:00 pm, 12 additional units had arrived, including two K-9 units. At 2:11 pm, gunshots were recorded on Ferguson Police logs and by the ambulance service, additional gunshots were recorded at 2:14 pm. The recorded gunshots resulted in an additional 20 units being sent to the area, including additional K-9 units and a SWAT team. At 3:30 pm, the scene was determined by police to be controlled enough to allow the medical examiner to examine Brown's body. Brown's body was transported to the morgue about 30 minutes later.

Michael Brown's friend who was with him that day provided another version of the encounter in interviews with the media and via social media. He indicated the two males were walking down the street when Officer Wilson drove by them and instructed them 'get the f$#@ on the sidewalk' and continued driving, that he and Brown replied they were 'not but a minute away from [their] destination, and [they] would shortly be out of the street', that Officer Wilson then stopped, reversed suddenly, and positioned his vehicle to block their path. Office Wilson attempted to 'open his door aggressively, but the car door ricocheted off their bodies causing it to close again, that Officer Wilson then grabbed Brown around his neck through the open window and Brown tried to pull away, but Wilson continued to pull on him 'like a tug of war', that Brown didn't try to reach for Officer Wilson's weapon and never struck him but was trying to get free, that when Officer Wilson drew his weapon he said, "I'll shoot you" or "I'm going to shoot" and fired the weapon striking Brown. That Brown got free and then started running away and that Officer Wilson exited the vehicle and began shooting at Brown as he fled, at his back as he chased him, that Brown stopped and turned toward Wilson and raised his arms saying, "I don't have a gun," was mad, and tried to say, "I don't have a gun" again but never got the sentence out because that's when Wilson shot Brown several more times. Johnson did not officially give a statement to St. Louis County Police until 13 August, four days after the incident. When Johnson gave his statement, he was accompanied by his mother, two attorneys, and a friend who indicated he was in charge of the personal security of Johnson.

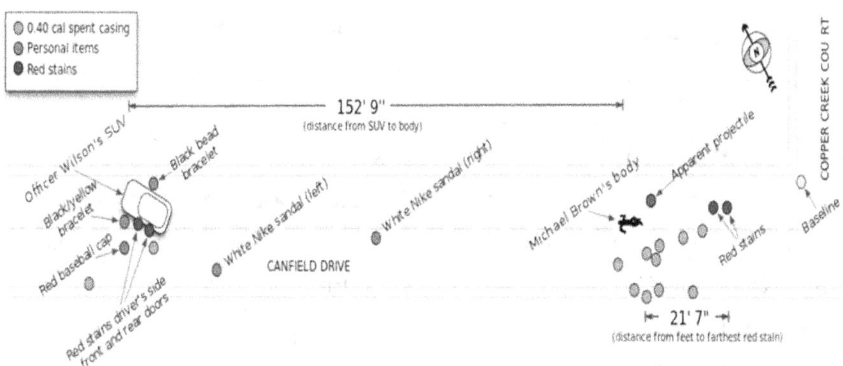

Diagram of the shooting scene found on wikipedia.org/wiki/killing_of_Michael_Brown Drawing by St. Louis County Police, Case #:2014-43984, of evidence collected at scene, documents submitted to Grand Jury during proceedings. Author: Cwobeel using Adobe Illustrator shared to Wikimedia Commons granting permission to copy, distribute, and/or modify the document under the terms of the GNU Free Documentation License, Version 1.2 or any later version. See cite and modify caption cite to:

https://en.wikipedia.org/wiki/File:Michael_Brown_shooting_scene_diagram.svg

Diagram compiled from multiple sources: *Documents Released in the Ferguson Case*. The New York Times (November 25, 2014). Archived from *the original* on 2014-12-05. Retrieved on December 5, 2014. (See *diagram* and *legend* in second row from bottom.); *What Happened in Ferguson? The New York Times* (November 25, 2014). Archived from *the original* on 2014-11-29. Retrieved on December 1, 2014; and Karklis, Laris (November 25, 2014). *What Ferguson police collected at the scene. The Washington Post*. Retrieved on December 4, 2014.

On the night of 9 August, protests and vigils in memory of Michael Brown were held. The television media and social media reports claimed that Michael Brown had his hands up and said 'Don't shoot' before Officer Wilson essentially executed him. One reported witness even stated that Michael Brown was on his knees with his hands up and pleading when Officer Wilson shot him at point-blank range. The reports indicated that Brown was repeatedly shot in the back as he fled from a confrontation with the officer that the officer had initiated.

Ferguson was a mostly minority community with a mostly white government and police department, there were already racial divisions in the neighborhood. Only a month earlier, the claims that Eric Garner had died at the hands of police using a 'chokehold' in New York were still resonating. Racial division and tensions were already high nationwide as the protests had only recently become less frequent and confrontational.

On 10 August, a candlelight vigil and memorial in honor of Michael Brown began peacefully but turned unruly later into the evening. Ferguson Police responded by turning out a force of about 150 officers dressed in full riot gear. The police attempted to disburse the crowd, but things got worse instead of better. Some people who were gathered started looting neighborhood stores, vandalizing vehicles, and confronting police who sought to block off access to certain areas of the city. Media covered the outbreak of the demonstrations and categorized it as over aggressive response by 'militarized' police using military-style weapons in response to civil disobedience.

The social media reports and media coverage inflamed an already tense situation and over the next several days, more protests and demonstrations occurred. On 11 August, the FBI reported that the Department of Justice (DOJ) was opening a Civil Rights investigation into the killing of Michael Brown by Officer Wilson. On 12 August, President Obama weighed in offering his condolences to the Brown family and the community. On 14 August, Senator Rand Paul of Kentucky said in a *Time Magazine* op-ed that the police needed to be demilitarized.

On 15 August, the Ferguson Police Department released the report and videotape footage of Michael Brown and Dorian Johnson inside the Ferguson Market committing the robbery followed by the confrontation between Brown and the store clerk. The Ferguson Police said they released the information because of legal requests under Missouri law by several media and social justice organizations. The Brown family released a statement condemning the Police Chief for the manner in which the footage was released, calling it character assassination following an 'execution-style murder' of their son. The Department of Justice had recommended keeping the footage out of the public warning it may enflame the situation. Missouri Governor Jay Nixon said the release was an attempt to disparage Brown during the investigation and would increase tensions in the community.

During the days following the incident, information concerning the case was released that contradicted information that had been previously released, especially by Ferguson Police. This only served to heighten tensions and support the narrative that the case was being handled to protect the officer, who must have been at fault for the killing. The Missouri Governor ordered that the Missouri State Police assume police responsibilities in Ferguson to quell further demonstrations and protests.

On 20 August, a previously empaneled Grand Jury of 12 persons, three Black, and nine White, was presented the evidence concerning the case. The racial makeup of the Grand Jury roughly matched the racial makeup of St. Louis County which is 70% White and 30% Black. The Grand Jury was instructed to review the evidence as an investigative Grand Jury, which is an abnormal process. The Grand Jury process is usually used to determine whether sufficient evidence exists to support probable cause to proceed to criminally charge a person. In this case, the Grand Jury received all the evidence, both against the officer and clearing the officer of wrongdoing. The elected County Prosecutor, Robert P. McCulloch, was in charge but did not present the evidence during the Grand Jury review. He indicated that the evidence would be released to the public if a finding of no indictment was made, another unusual decision in the process which is usually secretive.

Over the next three months, the Grand Jury heard evidence on the case. There were 60 witnesses presented, both supporting and contradicting Officer Wilson's testimony, who also testified. There were over 5,000 pages of transcribed testimony from the witnesses.

After 25 Grand Jury sessions and a considerable period of deliberation, the Grand Jury determined that Officer Wilson would not be indicted for the killing of Michael Brown. On the evening of 24 November, Prosecutor McCulloch held a 20-minute news conference announcing the Grand Jury findings. After the new conference, McCulloch released thousands of pages of

Grand Jury materials. The released documents included expert testimony, witness testimony, and transcripts of Grand Jury proceedings. The released information was made available for public review on the internet. On 8 and 13 December, additional Grand Jury evidence was released which included audio recordings of police dispatch and more witness interviews, including Dorian Johnson's interview.

The news of Officer Wilson not being indicted was not received well. Protests erupted in Ferguson and turned violent and destructive. Twenty-five businesses and buildings were burned to the ground. There was rampant looting and vandalism. Gunshots rang out throughout the city. Several police vehicles were destroyed and burned in the resulting melees. St. Louis County Police used tear gas canisters and rubber bullets against the protestors to disburse crowds. The protests weren't contained to Ferguson, protests spread in 170 cities across the United States.

On 4 March 2015, the Department of Justice (DOJ) released its findings on the death of Michael Brown. The DOJ review included detailed examinations of the evidence, a review of the legal statutes in Missouri concerning homicide and self-defense, the findings of three autopsies conducted on Michael Brown, and summaries of testimony from many witnesses. The FBI even performed over 300 additional interviews with potential witnesses who had not initially come forward due to fear of retaliation or other reasons, including distrust of the police. The DOJ determined that the evidence does not support the indictment of Officer Wilson in the death of Michael Brown.

The DOJ cited numerous witnesses whose testimony supported the version of events that closely mirrored the testimony of Officer Wilson. The DOJ report also noted that audio recordings of the gunshots also supported Officer Wilson. The autopsies concluded that Brown had not received any gunshot entry wounds on the back side of his body and that the final shot had struck Brown in the top of the head as he was falling forward toward Officer Wilson. Brown either fell due to the gunshot wounds to his chest which had punctured a lung or because his shorts had slid down while he ran causing him to trip. The evidence revealed that Brown's left hand, even though it was under his body, was balled into a fist after death. Brown's injured right hand was at his waistline near his right hip, palm up.

The DOJ report discounts many persons who had testified in opposition to Officer Wilson as they either gave false or inconsistent testimony or gave hearsay testimony. Ultimately, the DOJ determined these witness statements did not correlate with forensics or other witness accounts that were more consistent and credible. Some persons made witness statements even though they had no actual view of the incident and only heard about it 'from a friend who was there' or saw it on a media source. Dorian Johnson, the friend accompanying Brown that day, recanted his 'hand's up, don't shoot' statements and admitted, 'Big Mike' never did or said that.

The aftermath of the Ferguson Riots that took place after the death of Michael Brown and after the Grand Jury decision not to indict Officer Wilson resulted in additional pressures on law enforcement and efforts of reform. In December 2014, President Obama created a commission to make recommendations for broad police reforms across the United States.

The commission released its interim report on 2 March 2015, including a recommendation that a policy be created mandating 'external and independent criminal investigations in cases of police use of force resulting in death, officer-involved shootings resulting in injury or death, and in-custody deaths'. From a practical point of view, this would be virtually impossible. There are approximately 18,000 law enforcement agencies, large, medium, and small across the United States. How would this 'policy' be initiated, enforced, and carried out? The DOJ already serves this function with their oversight and investigative capabilities which were used in this case to serve as a full review of evidence for possible federal prosecution.

The DOJ launched an investigation into the Ferguson Police Department separate from the Michael Brown death on 4 September 2014. The DOJ investigation was intended to identify harms caused by the practices of the Ferguson Police Department so reforms could be implemented to improve community relations and interactions. The DOJ investigators reviewed documents, arrest records, citation issuance records, citizen contact data, interviewed community members and police personnel, accompanied officers on patrol during 'ride-alongs', and reviewed the city of Ferguson practices and policies. The conclusion, released on 4 March 2015, was that the Ferguson Police Department, and the city of Ferguson, emphasized revenue generation instead of public safety. Patrol assignments and schedules were directed toward municipal code enforcement, not crime prevention and public safety.

Officer's promotion possibilities and positive performance review results were based upon 'productivity', meaning citation issuance.

This created an atmosphere where officers viewed the public as potential offenders instead of persons deserving of service and protection. The culture within the police department emphasized strict compliance with police direction and an unwillingness by police personnel to see citizen's points of view or complaints as legitimate. That acts of a person exercising their First Amendment right to free speech was viewed as civil disobedience, resulting in arrest or citations. Police management did little to respond to citizen complaints of mistreatment, dispute, or excessive use of force against them.

The DOJ review also concluded that the Ferguson Municipal Court also contributed to this oppressive environment. That the court did not act as a neutral arbiter or check on police misconduct. Rather the court served as a process to issue fines, compel payments, and collections. When fines went unpaid, the court continued the process of revenue generation through warrant issuance. The court issued warrants of arrest for minor infractions such as traffic violations, parking infractions, and housing code violations. When fines weren't remitted, the court ordered the suspension of driver's licenses until fines were paid in full, contrary to Missouri law.

The Ferguson Police were also noted as being racially biased in their law enforcement activities. Although African Americans accounted for two-thirds of the population, they accounted for 90–95% of infractions and arrests. These numbers were generally for minor municipal code violations and traffic infractions. When the use of force was considered, 90% of the use of force cases were against African Americans. In the period reviewed by the DOJ, every K-9 bite incident occurred against an African American subject.

The report continued to highlight the disparate treatment of African American and minority populations within the city of Ferguson by the police and by the city government and Court. The city leaders responded to the complaints and problems reported by the citizens with indifference, saying the problem lay with certain segments of the population and their lack of 'personal responsibility'. All of this contributed to the atmosphere of distrust between the citizenry and the government officials of Ferguson. The report concluded with 13 recommended reforms for both the Ferguson Police Department and the Ferguson Municipal Court to initiate to improve the relationship between the citizens and the Ferguson governing bodies.

Michael Brown was one victim out of many in this incident. He was raised in the corrosive atmosphere of a racially divided city and governmental system. His behavior may have been based on this experience. We can look back and say that he was wrong in what he chose to do that day, we have that luxury. That it is his fault that he was shot and killed, but that would be prejudicial of us without knowing what he felt. His death was a tragedy that resulted from years of inappropriate governance and police practices. This may have been born of financial distress from the 'Great Recession' or it may be a horrible holdover from history. Either way, it never should have happened.

Other victims in the city of Ferguson were the residents and business owners who endured the violent demonstrations, riots, and destruction of their city. The innocent suffered because of the anger, frustration, and rage. The innocent suffered because of the political atmosphere, used by persons to forward their position, whatever that may be.

On 12 March 2015, Ferguson Police Chief Thomas Jackson resigned. On that same day at a protest outside the Ferguson Police Department, two officers were wounded by gunfire while they provided security. On 9 May 2016, the Chief of Ferguson Police position was filled by Delrish Moss, the first African American Police Chief in Ferguson's history who pledged to diversify the police force and improve community relations. Officer Darren Wilson resigned on 29 November 2015, after serving about four years in the Ferguson Police Department. He stated 'safety concerns' for his fellow officers as the reason for his resignation. The Prosecutor McCulloch was defeated in his re-election bid in 2018 by a wide margin, ending his 28-year career as the St. Louis County Prosecutor.

In December 2014, President Obama announced the federal government would make available $75 million to equip police officers with body cameras to provide more reliable evidence in police enforcement and use of force cases. Michael Brown's family settled a lawsuit against Officer Wilson, Chief Jackson, and the city of Ferguson in their claim for damages in a wrongful death case. Dorian Johnson also filed a lawsuit for violation of his Fourth Amendment rights based upon the DOJ's findings that the Ferguson Police targeted revenue in enforcement activities, but that suit was dismissed by the District Court after an Appellate Court reviewed it and directed the case dismissed.

Once again, popular culture emphasized the racial disparity and division in the society. Within the month after Brown's death, a group of American rap singers released a collaborative song entitled 'Don't Shoot' as a tribute. In November, a musician and filmmaker made the news after releasing a protest song following the Grand Jury verdict not to indict Wilson. The lyrics of the song were printed in the *Los Angeles Daily Times*. In 2015, following the death of Freddie Gray and the protests that happened after that incident, Prince released the song 'Baltimore', singing 'Does anybody hear us pray for Michael Brown or Freddie Gray?' Tributes in music and media continued through 2016 and 2017 from various artists and media outlets.

In 2020, the new St. Louis County Prosecutor, Wesley Bell, ordered a review of the case file renewing an effort to indict Officer Wilson in Brown's death. After a five-month review process, Bell announced he wouldn't be charging Wilson as he didn't 'have the evidence to ethically bring a charge against Darren Wilson'.

Caption: Protestors displaying 'Hands Up' signs in Ferguson, MO
https://en.wikipedia.org/wiki/Killing_of_Michael_Brown
Photograph taken by Jamelle Bouie and posted to Wikipedia under license CC BY 2.0 (terms listed here: *https://creativecommons.org/licenses/by/2.0/.*)

The phrase 'Hands Up, Don't Shoot' continues to echo and represent the racial disparity that existed in Ferguson and continues to exist in places, which contributed to the early tragic death of Michael Brown.

Chapter 12
2015

On 12 April 2015, about a month after the DOJ report on the death of Michael Brown was released announcing that the federal government would not seek civil rights actions against Officer Darren Wilson, another incident would occur involving a young unarmed Black male in police custody. This date was exactly one month from the day after Ferguson Police Chief Jackson's resignation and the demonstrations surrounding that announcement. This time, the young man would be inside a police transport vehicle, a 'paddy-wagon' in Baltimore, Maryland when the injuries contributing to his death would occur. The young man's death would come one week later, on 19 April 2015, in a hospital after he succumbed to his injuries. The cause of those injuries, while in police custody, would be one of the major mysteries that remain to be solved.

On the morning of 12 April, Baltimore City Police Lt. Brian Rice and Officers Edward Nero and Garrett Miller were performing bicycle-mounted patrol in the City of Baltimore. The officers were patrolling the area of Baltimore's Gilmor Homes housing project, an area known to have a high number of foreclosed homes, poverty, drug dealing, and violent crime. Three weeks prior, the State Prosecutor for the City of Baltimore, Marilyn Mosby, had requested 'enhanced' drug enforcement efforts near the intersection of West North Avenue and North Mount Street, in this neighborhood.

During their patrol of the area, Lt. Rice made eye contact with Freddie Gray, a 25-year-old Black male standing on the corner of an intersection. While the officer and Gray were looking at each other, Gray began running from the officers. After a brief chase, near Presbury and Mount, Gray surrendered to Officer Miller who had drawn his Taser device and warned Gray of its possible use. The officers frisked and handcuffed Gray, leading to their discovery of a spring-assisted knife clipped inside Gray's pocket. Officer Miller placed the knife on the ground and Gray attempted to move it, resulting in Miller repositioning Gray from a seated position on the sidewalk to a position lying on his stomach. Gray then started flailing his legs around, so Officer Miller placed Gray's legs into a 'leg lace' to control them.

A police transport vehicle, a 'paddy-wagon' arrived (see #1-'Arrest' on diagram on opposite page) to transport Gray which was driven by Officer Caesar Goodson. At this point, a small crowd of bystanders had gathered and angrily protested Gray's arrest. As officers attempted to load Gray into the transport van, he yelled about his wrists and 'went limp' allowing his legs to drag. Officers moved him to the rear of the vehicle where he stood and stepped up into the vehicle using his legs. Gray was placed on a bench on the right side of the transport vehicle without being seat-belted in place. The vehicle had a hard partition running down the centerline of the vehicle separating the left and right sides. Once Gray was inside and the doors shut, witnesses could hear Gray inside the vehicle banging against the walls and yelling. Lt. Rice directed the driver, Officer Goodson, to meet them at a nearby location (#2-'Stop 1' on diagram) so they could resecure Gray with leg shackles and get clear from the crowd of bystanders for the officer's safety.

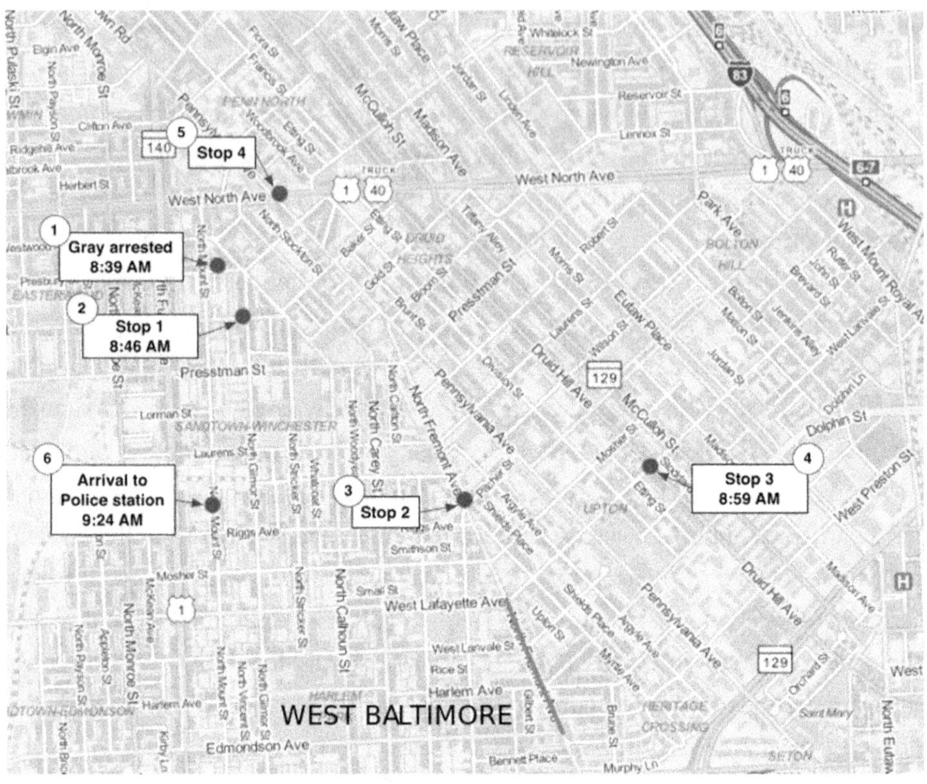

Map of West Baltimore area showing Gray's arrest and transport route to Police station from Wikipedia

Wikipedia User: Cwobeel, permission granted to use under license CC BY-SA 4.0 (license available here: *https://creativecommons.org/licenses/by-sa/4.0/*). No changes made from original. Info compiled by Cwobeel using information published in:
https://www.nytimes.com/interactive/2015/04/30/us/what-happened-freddie-gray-arrested-by-baltimore-police-department-map-timeline.html;
https://en.wikipedia.org/wiki/Killing_of_Freddie_Gray#/media/File:Timeline_of_Freddie_Gray's_arrest.svg

One block away (#2-'Stop 1' on diagram), the transport vehicle stopped and met the arresting officers. When officers attempted to remove Gray from the vehicle, he resisted. Gray was pulled out of the vehicle, flailing and yelling. While officers were placing new restraints on Gray, another crowd assembled and angrily yelled at the officers about the arrest. Some claimed that the officers had injured Gray. Officer William Porter performed crowd control while the arresting officers were restraining Gray. Once secured, officers attempted to reload Gray into the transport wagon, but he again 'went limp' refusing to walk or assist his movement. To load Gray, officers had to lift him into the vehicle and load him headfirst on his stomach. Lt. Rice entered the transport vehicle and lifted from Gray's shoulders while Officer Miller lifted his legs. Officers slid Gray into the vehicle and left him on his stomach on the compartment floor, head facing the front of the vehicle, again unseat-belted. Again, once the doors were closed, witnesses and officers could hear Gray yelling and banging against the walls of the transport wagon, causing it to shake. The driver was instructed to take Gray to central booking, so the driver left in that direction.

Officer Goodson, driving the vehicle, made a brief unplanned stop while driving to the central booking (#3-'Stop 2' on diagram), exited the vehicle, and walked toward the rear of the vehicle. It is unknown what prompted this or what happened at this time as there is no video evidence and Goodson refused to answer questions concerning this. What is known is that he re-entered the vehicle several seconds later and radioed for a police unit to meet him at Druid Hill and Dolphin Street (#4-'Stop 3' on diagram) to check on Gray's condition.

Officer Porter responded to Officer Goodson's request and met the transport wagon just north of the intersection of Druid Hill and Dolphin. When Officer Porter arrived, he met Officer Goodson at the rear of the vehicle and Goodson opened the doors unprompted. Gray was lying on his stomach head toward the front of the vehicle, handcuffed and shackled. Gray asked for 'help' and Officer Porter asked generally what was wrong with him. Gray then again said, "Help. Help me up." Officer Porter then entered the wagon and lifted Gray onto the bench into a seated position. Officer Porter asked if Gray wanted to go to the hospital and he responded yes. Gray sat unsupported and normally on the bench. He did not complain of any injuries or pain and did not show any outward signs of injury.

Officer Porter advised the driver that although Gray didn't show any signs of injury, he wouldn't 'pass medical' at central booking so he directed the driver to take Gray straight to the hospital. Immediately after this Lt. Rice requested available units and a transport vehicle to respond to a nearby location. Officers Porter and Goodson both responded to Lt. Rice's call and each left in their vehicles to the location. Although Gray was seated on the bench at this time, he was again not secured with a seatbelt on the bench.

Approximately, four minutes later the vehicles arrived at Lt. Rice's location (#5-'Stop 4' on diagram). Lt. Rice and Officers Nero and Miller had another suspect in custody and needed him loaded into the transport to be taken to the Western District Station for questioning. While loading the new suspect in the transport wagon, an officer noticed Gray now in a crouched position on his knees leaning on the bench with his arms, described as in 'a praying position'. Baltimore PD Sergeant Alicia White was present and seeing Gray in this position, asked him some questions but received no direct responses, only an audible noise in response.

Officer Porter again asked Gray if he wanted to go to the hospital and Gray responded, "Yes." Sergeant White directed Goodson to take the new suspect to Western District Station and then Gray to the hospital. Sgt. White directed Porter to follow the transport wagon and escort Gray to the hospital thereafter. Several minutes later the transport wagon arrived at the Western District Station (#6-Arrival at Police Station on diagram). The new suspect indicated there was nothing unusual about the ride to the station, there were no sudden stops or starts, violent turns, or anything remarkable and it was a smooth ride. He further indicated he could hear a loud banging on the center partition which he thought may have been someone banging their head against the wall. When the officers arrived at the Western District Station, Gray was found unconscious, eyes shut, neck limp, and he appeared to not be breathing. Sergeant White noted that Gray was drooling.

Paramedics were called and upon arrival, found Gray to be unconscious, with a small amount of blood running from his nose, and a frothy vomitus discharge around his mouth. Gray was transported to the hospital by paramedics where he was determined to be comatose. Testing and diagnoses revealed Gray had a fractured neck and pinched spinal cord. His injuries were described as comparable to those sustained when a person strikes their head diving into a shallow pool or water area. Efforts, including surgery, were performed to attempt to aid Gray, but he succumbed to medical complications resulting from his injuries on 19 April 2015.

The officers involved in the arrest and transport of Gray were all placed on paid administrative leave pending an investigation. On 1 May 2015, the medical examiner's report was provided to the investigators indicating that Gray's death was a homicide. State Attorney Mosby responded by saying they had probable cause to arrest the officers involved in Gray's case. Attorney Mosby charged the officers with multiple offenses including false imprisonment, three officers with manslaughter, and one with second-degree depraved-heart murder. The officers were also charged with various other lesser charges, including aggravated assault. The assault charges were added because the officers failed to follow department policy to seatbelt suspects during transport. That policy had only been enacted six days before this event.

As with the death of Michael Brown the year before, the common story was that Gray's death was the result of police excessive use of force. During his arrest and ensuing transport, Gray had demonstrated by yelling and flailing about. He had resisted the arrest by refusing to walk, going limp, and verbally proclaiming he did nothing wrong. At both the place of his initial arrest and during the period when he was unloaded from the vehicle to secure his legs, crowds had gathered, yelled at the police, and videotaped the processes. That footage had already been made public on social media and through print and television news organizations. The images showed how Gray was treated and the public perception was already formed. On 18 April 2015, hundreds of people gathered outside the Baltimore Police Department to protest Gray's treatment. On 21 April, two days after Gray's death, another protest occurred.

On 25 April 2015, a protest in downtown Baltimore was organized and it turned violent with protestors throwing rocks at police and setting fires. Many of the protestors were students who had been removed from city buses and told to disperse from the city.

Following this riot, 15 officers were injured and 34 people were arrested. On the day of Gray's funeral, 27 April, another violent protest occurred injuring another 15 officers, destroying two patrol vehicles, and burning several businesses, including a CVS Pharmacy.

The protest caused the Baltimore Orioles game to be rescheduled. In reaction to the violent protests, Maryland State Police sent 82 officers to assist. The Maryland Governor declared a state of emergency and activated the Maryland National Guard as well as 500 Maryland State Police Officers. The governor also requested an additional 5,000 officers from other area departments to be available if needed. A curfew from 10 pm to 5 am was enacted in the city. Baltimore City Schools and the University of Maryland-Baltimore campus were closed as was a major shopping mall complex as social media posts were encouraging 'purging', meaning violence as in the film series.

The violent protests and destruction continued throughout the next several days. Small businesses owned by Korean, Chinese, and Arab Americans were specifically targeted. Over 40 Korean-owned businesses were looted and destroyed. Gangs helped target and direct the attacks upon the businesses. Throughout the demonstrations, 27 pharmacies and 2 methadone clinics were looted and destroyed, believed to be intentionally targeted for the drugs that were sold on the streets and on the black market. By 2 May, the protest violence and destruction of property began to wane, and a large peaceful protest was held. On 3 May, the National Guard started withdrawing from Baltimore and the curfew was lifted. By 4 May, the National Guard had completely withdrawn from the city. Like before, the protests and demonstrations were not limited to the city where the event had occurred. Protests and demonstrations were held across multiple cities in the United States, from the east to the west coasts.

On 2 September 2015, it was determined that the officers charged in Freddie Gray's death would be tried individually in court. On 8 September 2015, the Baltimore Mayor, Stephanie Rawlings-Blake, announced a $6.4 million settlement to Gray's family. The mayor said the settlement shouldn't be viewed 'as a judgment on the guilt or innocence of the officers facing trial'. She continued it was just to avoid expensive and protracted litigation in the future. The Gray family had not even filed suit yet.

The first officer tried, Officer Porter, went to trial in December 2015. The jury was unable to reach a verdict and the judge, Barry Williams, declared a mistrial. The case was rescheduled for a new trial in September 2016. In May 2016, Officer Nero went to trial and was found not guilty on all charges in a bench trial again before Judge Williams. On 23 June 2016, Officer Goodson was acquitted of all charges in a bench trial as well. On 26 July 2016, Lt. Rice went to trial and was acquitted of all charges. On 27 July 2016, Officer Miller was scheduled to begin his trial. At a pre-trial hearing, all charges against Officers Miller, Nero, and Porter, whose trial in December had ended in a hung jury, were dismissed. The officers, three of which were African American, one of those being female, and three white, had all been cleared of criminal wrongdoing in Freddie Gray's death.

As in previous cases of possible excessive force by police, the Department of Justice (DOJ) initiated an investigation for possible violations of Freddie Gray's civil rights against the officers. The DOJ conducted a thorough review of all evidence including video footage, cell phone footage, witness interviews, forensic evidence review, and review of autopsy findings as well as departmental policies and procedures. The investigators reviewed legal issues both federally and under Maryland law. On 12 September 2017, the DOJ issued its findings and determined there was no evidence to sustain civil rights violation prosecutions against any of the officers involved in Freddie Gray's tragic death.

Once again, the popular culture picked up on the death and memorialized it in song and film. HBO produced a documentary called 'Baltimore Rising' about Freddie Gray's death and the protests that followed. Various other artists also reference Freddie Gray in their lyrics.

Another victim of the aftermath was the Baltimore citizenry. Besides the many businesses that were looted and destroyed during the protests, Baltimore experienced a serious rise in violent crime. Some of this was a result of the looted drugs available after the demonstrations, but there was also reportedly a confidence increase by those seeking to act criminally. The police were held back, they were hesitant to act. The police responded to the charges against the officers by curtailing their activities in high-crime areas of the city to minimize risk to themselves, physically and legally. One resident commented, "Before it was over-policing, now there's no police," in the neighborhood. The officers indicated they were 'confused and unsupported' by the city and management. Every time they went to make an arrest, they were surrounded by 30–50 people, yelling, and recording them. The police became 'afraid of going to jail for doing their jobs properly'. One officer commented anonymously, "After the protests, it seems the citizens would appreciate a lack of police presence, that's exactly what they're getting." By the end of 2015, Baltimore would experience 344 homicides, a 50% reduction in arrests, and a spike in other violent crimes including shooting incidents. The 344 homicides were the second highest on record and the first time since 1999 that there were more than 300.

Chapter 13
2016

On 5 July and 6 July 2016, there were two police shootings which would again cause outrage and result in protests and violent demonstrations. In each of these cases, the victims of the shootings would have firearms in their possession at the time of their encounter with law enforcement. The question would be why the police officers reacted so swiftly and resorted to the use of deadly force. Unfortunately, like with Eric Garner and Michael Brown, retaliatory attacks against police would follow, costing more lives.

In the early morning hours just after midnight on 5 July 2016, Alton Sterling was outside the Triple S Food Mart in Baton Rouge, Louisiana selling CDs when police were called to the scene. Police 911 dispatch received an anonymous call reporting a Black man wearing a red shirt and selling CDs had threatened him with a gun. The call disconnected but the caller called again a few minutes later and completed giving the information to police dispatch. The caller had reported that the suspect had pulled the gun out of his pocket. Dispatch notified two Baton Rouge police officers of the call and they proceeded to the location. The officers arrived at the location and approached Sterling, a 37-year-old Black man matching the description given by the caller. As police arrived, they saw Sterling gathering up his CDs and possibly trying to place them into a nearby vehicle. After the next 90 seconds had passed, Alton Sterling, 'CD Man' as he was known locally, would be dead from multiple gunshots after a struggle with the officers.

The officers dispatched to the scene are identified as Howie Lake II and Blane Salamoni. Officer Lake had three years of experience in law enforcement; Salamoni had four years. Officer Lake had been involved in a previous shooting incident when a fleeing suspect crashed his vehicle into a house and then engaged in a shoot-out with six officers who were pursuing him at the time. That suspect was wounded during the exchange of gunfire. Sterling also had a history, including a prior resisting arrest charge where he had a gun in his possession for which he served five years in prison and other violent offenses. The history of the subjects involved is important because that can influence the behavior of the participants.

Upon arrival, Officer Lake ordered Sterling to stop moving and put his hands on the car. Officer Lake quickly approached Sterling near the table Sterling had set up and politely asked a woman to move saying, "Excuse me, Ma'am." He then addressed Sterling stating, "Do me a favor and put your hands on the car real quick." Sterling responded to the officer saying something and started to move toward the table, Officer Lake placed his left hand on Sterling's right upper torso near the armpit and said, "Stop, stop." Sterling responded with not sure what he was talking about and continued to try to move away. Officer Lake repeated the command to place his hands on the car quickly and grabbed Sterling's right arm turning Sterling to face the car and Sterling asked what was this about. At this time, Sterling and Officer Lake began to struggle for control; Lake trying to hold Sterling down on the hood of the vehicle.

Officer Salamoni assisted Lake grabbing Sterling's neck and then drew his weapon and pointed it at Sterling's head. Sterling asked, "What I did?" Officer Salamoni told Sterling, "Put your hands on the car or I'll shoot you in the f$#@ing head." Sterling complied and placed his hands on the car hood. Seconds later, Sterling again tried to raise his hands from the hood. Salamoni then said, "Tase his a$$" and the officers backed away. Officer Lake drew his Taser device and attempted to incapacitate Sterling. Sterling briefly dropped to his knees and then stood back up facing the officers. Lake again activated his Taser device which had no effect.

The officers tackled Sterling with Officer Salamoni on Sterling's torso and Lake on Sterling's thighs. Sterling was on his back; however, his right arm and hand were still free. Sterling and the officers were on the ground near the front driver's side of a vehicle with Sterling's right shoulder and arm underneath the vehicle as officers attempted to control the arm. Throughout the struggle, the officers repeated the command to get on the ground to Sterling. Officer Salamoni then yelled, "He's going for his pocket, he's got a gun! Gun!" Officer Salamoni again yelled, "Going for the gun," and he drew his weapon and fired three shots into Sterling's chest. Officer Lake, who had stood up and drawn his weapon, was pointing it at Sterling and commanded Sterling to 'stay on the ground'.

Officer Salamoni rolled off Sterling after firing the three rounds. Salamoni was now on his back facing Sterling's back. Sterling continued to move and began to sit up rolling to his left. Sterling brought his right arm across his torso and toward the ground. Officer Lake repeated the command to 'get on the ground'. At this time, Officer Salamoni fired three additional rounds into Sterling's back. Sterling lay back and Officer Lake reached into Sterling's right pocket and removed a fully loaded .38 caliber revolver. Officer Lake then announces shots fired on his radio, calls for additional units to the scene, and requests emergency medical services.

Following the shooting, Officer Lake directed all the bystanders to stay put so they could provide witness statements. Both officers provided statements concerning the shooting. The investigators collected video footage from the store's camera system, cell phone footage, body camera footage, and evidence from the scene.

On the night of 5 July 2016, over 100 protestors gathered in an intersection in Baton Rouge and blocked traffic. The protestors shouted, "No justice, no peace," and fired off fireworks during the protest. Police were called in to disperse the crowd of approximately 200 persons and reopen the roadway to traffic. The protestors went to reorganize in front of City Hall.

The following day, 6 July 2016, in the St. Paul suburb of Falcon Heights, Minnesota, another tragic death would occur after a police shooting. A little over 1,200 miles due North of Baton Rouge, Philando Castile was driving his vehicle when he was stopped by police looking for suspects involved in a recent robbery in the area. Castile was accompanied by his girlfriend, Diamond Reynolds, and her four-year-old daughter who was in the backseat.

At about 9:00 pm, Officer Jeronimo Yanez with the St. Anthony Police Department radioed a nearby officer that he was going to stop a vehicle to identify the occupants as they looked a lot like the descriptions given of suspects in an earlier robbery. The other officer, Joseph Kauser, responded saying he would assist him at the stop. Officer Yanez responded that he would wait until the other squad was there and told Officer Kauser that the driver had a wide-set nose which matched the robbery suspect's description. Both officers had four years of experience with the St. Anthony Police Department.

Officer Yanez initiated the stop on Castile's vehicle and approached Castile on the driver's side of the vehicle. Officer Kauser approached the passenger side of the vehicle. Officer Yanez asked for Castile's license and proof of insurance information. Castile handed Officer Yanez the insurance information and told Officer Yanez, "Sir, I do have to tell you that I have a firearm on me." Officer Yanez replied, "Ok," and placed his right hand on the holster with his weapon.

Officer Yanez then said to Castile, "Okay, don't reach for it, and then…don't pull it out."

Castile responded, "I'm not pulling it out," and Reynolds, in the passenger seat, also said, "He's not pulling it out."

Yanez, raising his voice said, "Don't pull it out!" as he quickly drew his weapon and reached inside the driver's window with his left hand. Reynolds then screamed "No," and Yanez withdrew his left hand from the car and fired seven shots at Yanez, striking him five times. Approximately, 40 seconds had passed since Yanez had started talking with Castile through the car window. Reynolds yelled, "You just killed my boyfriend" as Castile leaned forward on the steering wheel moaning, "I wasn't reaching for it."

Reynolds said, "He wasn't reaching for it" and Yanez repeated the command, "Don't pull it out."

Reynolds responded, "He wasn't."

Then Yanez yelled, "Don't move, F$#@."

Several seconds after the shots were fired, Ms. Reynolds used her phone to start streaming the event using Facebook Live, a relatively new feature on Facebook. The ten-minute live video begins with Castile leaning over the steering wheel, moaning, and still moving with a bloody left arm and side. Reynolds was speaking with Officer Yanez saying that Castile had a license to carry and that was why he had a firearm, that Castile had told the officer that his wallet was in his pocket but that he had a pistol on him. Reynolds then says the officer told him, "Don't move" and that when Castile brought his hands up, the officer shot him four or five times. Reynolds continued saying, "You shot him and all he was doing was getting his license and registration." Then she said, "Please don't tell me he's dead."

Officer Yanez was heard excitedly saying, "I told him not to reach for it. I told him to get his hands open!"

Once outside the vehicle, Reynolds was ordered to her knees by another officer and her phone dropped to the ground but continued recording. Reynolds was handcuffed and placed into Officer Kauser's vehicle with her daughter. Officer Kauser's dash cam video recorded Reynold's daughter saying, "Mom, please stop cussing and screaming 'cause I don't want you to get shooted." Reynolds was transported to the station and released after questioning at 5:00 am on 7 July.

A little after midnight on 7 July, peaceful but angry protestors gathered at the scene of Castile's death. More than 200 people gathered near that location, laying flowers and other memorials.

Another group of protestors gathered at the Minnesota Governor's residence in nearby St. Paul.

Those protestors chanted Castile's name and demanded that the Minnesota Governor, Mark Dayton, make a statement. The protests continued, 'peaceful but forceful', and later that morning the governor made a statement offering condolences, promising a complete investigation, and saying justice would be served. Governor Dayton also made the comment asking, "Would this have happened if those passengers would have been white? I don't think it would have." Governor Dayton then called for a State-led investigation into the matter.

On 7 July 2016, in Dallas, Texas, as well as in many other cities across the United States, protests and demonstrations against police excessive force and racial bias were organized after the killings of Sterling and Castile. President Obama, without commenting specifically on the cases, said, "Americans should feel outraged at episodes of police brutality since they're rooted in long-simmering racial discord." The New Orleans Field Office of the FBI issued a warning about 'threats to law enforcement and potential threats to the safety of the general public' stemming from Sterling's death in Baton Rouge. The warning would be too late.

Micah Johnson, a 25-year-old Black male, an Army Reserve Afghan War veteran, dressed in military gear, parked his Sport Utility Vehicle (SUV) on Lamar Street in front of Building A of El Centro College in Dallas. About 800 persons were marching nearby and the route would pass this location on Main Street. At 8:58 pm, Johnson opened fire on police and bystanders, targeting white police officers. Three officers were immediately killed by the rifle fire, and several more were injured along with a civilian bystander. An officer appeared near a corner behind Johnson drawn by the gunfire. The officer and Johnson exchanged gunfire. Johnson was wounded in this exchange, but his firing caused the officer to take cover behind a cement pillar. Johnson fired at one side of the pillar then the other to pin the officer down, then flanked him and shot him in the back several times, killing him.

Johnson then entered El Centro College through a shot-out window, moved to the second floor, and fired down at other officers, killing a fifth officer. Johnson continued to exchange gunfire with police, shooting through the sheetrock walls with his rifle keeping the police at a distance. Johnson was eventually cornered in a large server room with only two exits. A police negotiator attempted to get Johnson to surrender; however, Johnson continued his rants yelling black power and calling for a revolution, asking the Black officer to turn his weapon on white officers, among other things. Johnson was killed when a police explosive disposal robot was equipped with an explosive charge which was detonated on the opposite side of the wall from Johnson, finally ending the stand-off at 2:30 am on 8 July. The final body count in Dallas was five officers killed, nine officers and two civilians wounded, and Johnson, the shooter, killed.

Demonstrations and protests continued throughout the United States, peaceful but disruptive. A large protest involving over 1,000 persons blocked Interstate Highways in Oakland, California. A representative of the United Nations Working Group of Experts on People of African Descent issued a statement condemning the killings and saying that they demonstrate a 'high level of structural and institutional racism'. The Bahamian government issued a travel advisory to their citizens warning young Black males to act responsibly if confronted by American police for any reason, urging them not to resist and avoid large gatherings and protests for their safety.

From 9 and 10 July, protests turned violent in both Baton Rouge and St. Paul. In Baton Rouge, one officer was injured and over 102 were arrested during the violence. In St. Paul, 15 officers were injured when protestors threw rocks, bottles, and Molotov cocktails (firebombs) at police. Protestors also blocked Interstate 94 leading into St. Paul. Police used tear gas and pepper spray to disperse the crowd and another 102 protestors were arrested.

On 17 July in Baton Rouge, Gavin Long, a 26-year-old Black male from Kansas City, Missouri, apparently went looking to target police in the area near the Hammond Mall. Long's motivations were unclear however he was described as a 'Black separatist' by law enforcement officials. Long was a decorated U.S. Marine who had served in Iraq and was under treatment for post-traumatic stress disorder (PTSD). Long's social media profiles claimed that he associated with several African American-based sovereign citizen movements. On 17 July at 8:40 am, police dispatch received a call regarding a suspicious man dressed in a long coat carrying a rifle in the area. Officers were sent to question the subject however due to Louisiana's open carry law had no probable cause to arrest him. As Baton Rouge police officers approached Long near the back of a beauty supply store, he opened fire on them, killing one and wounding the other, an East Baton Rouge Parish Deputy Sheriff attempted to help the wounded officer and was killed by gunfire from Long.

Long then approached the injured officer and shot him twice more, killing him. Long turned and seeing another officer near another store shot that officer. As he left that area, he saw two sheriff's deputies near his vehicle and he shot those deputies as well, wounding them. Responding officers exchanged gunfire with Long at 8:46 am and at 8:48 am, a SWAT officer shot and killed Long. One of the sheriff's deputies injured near his vehicle died of his injuries in 2022.

On 7 July, the United States Department of Justice (DOJ) opened a Civil Rights investigation into the death of Alton Sterling in Baton Rouge. On 2 May 2017, the DOJ announced that it would not be charging the officers involved in Sterling's shooting. The DOJ report states that the officers had been fighting with Sterling, attempted less-than-lethal force devices, that Sterling was larger and stronger than either officer or that the officers knew that Sterling had a firearm in his possession at the time, that based upon the totality of the circumstances (language from Graham v. Connor in Chapter 4) the use of deadly force was not unreasonable in this matter. Following the DOJ's announcement, the Louisiana attorney general announced the matter would be reviewed for State criminal violations. In March 2018, the autopsy report was released indicating Sterling had died of gunshot wounds but also noted that Sterling had intoxicating substances in his system at the time of the incident.

On 17 March, the State of Louisiana announced it wouldn't be prosecuting the officers for any violation of State law. On 30 March, Officer Salamoni was fired for violations of police use of force policies, and Officer Lake was suspended for three days for losing his temper during the encounter, being unprofessional. In 2021, the East Baton Rouge Metro Council approved a $4.5 million settlement in the wrongful death suit brought by Sterling's family.

In the case of Philando Castile's death, The Minnesota Bureau of Criminal Apprehension conducted the investigation and turned the evidence over to the Ramsey County Attorney for consideration of prosecution on 28 September 2016. Officer Yanez was charged with second-degree manslaughter and two counts of dangerous discharge of a firearm under Minnesota law. Yanez's trial for causing the death of Castile began on 30 May 2017. The jury in the case deliberated for more than 25 hours over five days. The jury of seven men and five women, with two Black members in the jury, found Officer Yanez not guilty on the charges. A jury person indicated that the largest issue was the lack of evidence which could definitively indicate that Castile didn't reach for the weapon in his possession at the time. The St. Anthony Police Department, a small department with 25 members, didn't have body cameras for their officers at the time. Dash camera footage didn't capture the necessary evidence and the Facebook Live video didn't capture the pre-shooting events.

Following the verdict, Officer Yanez was released from the St. Anthony Police Department. A large protest of approximately 2,000 persons gathered and marched in the streets, blocking traffic on Interstate 94 once again. In June 2017, the Castile family reached a settlement with the City of St. Anthony for $2.995 million in the wrongful death suit. The family established a Memorial Scholarship in Castile's name at the South St. Paul High School which he had attended. They also established the Philando Castile Relief Foundation which pays the outstanding school lunch balances of students at schools within the St. Paul School District, and nearby areas, and works toward reducing gun violence. Philando Castile was a Nutrition Services Supervisor at J.J. Hill Montessori Magnet School at the time of his death.

The Department of Justice was invited to review the St. Anthony Police Department policies and practices because of this event. The invitation came from the St. Anthony Police Chief and the councils of the three small St. Paul suburbs which the department served. The program of review and collaboration was part of the DOJ's Office of Community Policing Services. Unfortunately, the program was ended by the DOJ in 2017 before a complete review and recommendations for reforms were issued.

Chapter 14
March 2020

Throughout the remainder of 2017 and through 2018 and 2019, incidents of police use of force against persons of minority descent continued. Each time an incident occurred, social, television, and print media would again cover the incidents, and protests and demonstrations would result. Throughout this period, the language and emotions would continue to become more belligerent and volatile, building the angst between the police and the citizenry they are charged to protect and serve. On 13 March 2020, in Louisville, Kentucky, an incident occurred that would highlight the growing issue of law enforcement misconduct in the United States. The public protests and demonstrations that accompanied previous incidents were muted this time because of the COVID-19 pandemic. The world was learning to deal with the outbreak that was spreading quickly, governments had issued strict restrictions on the movement of citizens, especially large gatherings. These restrictions and the fear of the dangerous viral outbreak prevented immediate reaction following this incident.

At 12:40 am on 13 March, plainclothes police officers of the Louisville Metro Police Department (LMPD) served a 'no-knock' warrant on the apartment occupied by Breonna Taylor. The purpose of a 'no-knock' warrant is to allow the police the surprise of sudden entry into an occupied building when there is a potential risk to the officers if a 'knock and announce' type warrant is utilized. Even though police were issued a no-knock warrant in this case, they purportedly did knock and announce their presence prior to making a forced entry into the apartment with the use of a battering ram to open the door. As the officers entered the room after breaching the apartment door, Breonna Taylor's boyfriend, Kenneth Walker, fired at what he believed was an intruder, or intruders attempting to break into the residence. His shot struck one officer and the officers returned fire at Walker. Walker was not hit during the exchange however Ms. Taylor, standing behind Walker, was struck several times causing her death.

Following the incident, Walker was arrested for assault and attempted murder of a police officer, and Taylor's body was removed from the scene. The charges against Walker were dismissed in June of 2021 with prejudice, meaning they couldn't be brought again.

Although the purpose of the police obtaining the warrant was to search Taylor's apartment for possible drugs and drug proceeds, the apartment was never searched for these purposes. Police investigators had developed information that they had used to obtain the warrant which alleged that Taylor's former boyfriend, Jamarcus Glover, had been involved in drug trafficking and had used the apartment to store and conceal drugs and/or proceeds. Jamarcus Glover had been involved with a partner in the alleged drug trafficking who was identified as Adrian Walker, no relation to Kenneth Walker. Apparently, Glover and Taylor had been in an on-and-off relationship that began in 2016 and ended in February 2020. Glover had used Taylor's address on several occasions on bank records and for mailings. In 2016, a person was found shot to death in a vehicle that Glover had been using that Taylor had rented. Another person was convicted of the murder in that case.

After the shooting of Breonna Taylor, no officers were charged in her death. An investigation was opened into the incident and the officers were placed on administrative reassignment pending the investigation. Initially, Kenneth Walker stated that Taylor had fired the shot that had struck the officer, but he soon reversed that, admitting he fired the shot. Walker made a statement that Taylor had asked, 'Who is it?' referring to the loud banging at the door but Walker didn't respond and called his mother instead of 911 and armed himself with a firearm. The coroner determined Taylor's death was the result of multiple gunshots to the torso and denied releasing the autopsy report to the media. The department's internal Professional Integrity Unit conducted the investigation and turned over its findings to the Attorney General of Kentucky on 20 May 2020. The Louisville Mayor also requested that the FBI and U.S. Attorney's Office review the findings.

Following the investigation, Louisville Mayor Greg Fischer requested that Officer Brett Hankison, who was involved in the shooting, be removed from the Louisville Police Merit Board, which serves as a disciplinary review board.

This board is comprised of three citizens and two officers appointed by the River City Fraternal Order of Police.

On 19 June, Officer Hankison was notified that he was being terminated for 'wantonly and blindly' firing 10 rounds into Taylor's apartment. During the incident, Officer Hankison had moved outside the apartment building after the attempted entry and fired through a patio door and a window which were covered by blackout fabric and blinds. This meant he couldn't see into the apartment or if there were any threats inside. Hankison's rounds passed through Taylor's apartment and into a neighboring apartment where a family of three was residing. Hankison's actions were determined to be in violation of the department's use of force policy and he was terminated on 23 June. The other officers involved in the shooting, Jonathan Mattingly, who had been shot in the thigh by Walker, and Myles Cosgrove, who never entered the residence and fired from the doorway, remained on reassignment.

On 21 May 2020, the Louisville Office of the FBI opened its own independent investigation into the death of Breonna Taylor and the events surrounding the shooting. The FBI's investigation, as well as the internal investigation, would reveal much about the events leading up to this incident. During that same month, the Louisville Metro Police Department indicated it would change the policy requiring all officers to wear body cameras during warrant service duties. The LMPD would also change its warrant service processes and permanently suspend the use of 'no-knock' warrants. In mid-September 2020, Taylor's family resolved a wrongful death lawsuit for $12 million against the Louisville Metro Police Department.

On 23 September 2020, a state Grand Jury indicted Hankison on three counts of criminal wanton endangerment for endangering the lives of the persons in the neighboring apartment. The Grand Jury was not presented with charges of homicide to consider against Hankison or any other officer involved in the shooting. The officers had fired a total of 32 shots during the encounter, 6 by Mattingly, 16 by Cosgrove, including the fatal shots to Ms. Taylor, and 10 by Hankison from outside the apartment through the glass door and window. The shots hit many different parts of the apartment besides Taylor, and several passed through into the neighboring apartment and through the ceiling into the apartment above. Following the announcement of the charges, protests broke out as there were no charges of homicide for Taylor's death and no charges for endangerment of Black residents in the apartment above

Taylor's. The only charges brought were for endangerment of the residents in the apartment next door to Taylor's, who were white.

Several days later, racial tensions increased when a member of the Grand Jury criticized the state Attorney General for not presenting charges of homicide as a possibility and accused the Attorney General of using the Grand Jury to deflect 'accountability and responsibility' in the case. A second Grand Juror echoed these criticisms in October of 2020 saying the jury members were steered away from homicide charges and not instructed about self-defense laws during their deliberations. Some Grand Jury members felt that the police had 'covered it up' and 'didn't agree that certain actions were justified'.

On 4 August 2022, the Department of Justice released the results of its investigation. The FBI charged four officers, Hankison, and three officers who were instrumental in obtaining the warrant for the search with federal charges related to the shooting. Hankison, who had been acquitted during the State case for wanton endangerment was charged with federal civil rights violations in the case of Taylor and Walker in Taylor's residence and for the three persons in the neighboring apartment. The other charges were against officers who had obtained the warrant through falsification of reports and evidence and conspiracy to commit the same. The investigation had revealed that Officers Joshua Jayne and Kyle Meany had falsified an affidavit claiming they had obtained information concerning possible drug trafficking activity at Taylor's residence among other false statements. Another officer, Kelly Goodlett was charged with conspiracy in aiding Jaynes and Meany and participating in filing a false police report after the shooting which attempted to provide validity to the affidavit used to support the warrant issuance. Goodlett pleaded guilty to those charges on 23 August 2022 and was expected to testify at trial against the other officers. The federal investigation noted that the officers involved in serving the warrant were unaware that the warrant had been obtained using falsified information.

As with other incidents, the death of Breonna Taylor elicited protests concerning racial differences within the United States. The quarantines and lockdowns related to the COVID-19 pandemic muted the initial public demonstrations, but that did nothing to alleviate the anguish of the people who endured the racially disparate treatment. Several actions were taken legislatively to address the problems with police use of 'no-knock' warrants including the Justice in Policing Act of 2020 which addressed misconduct, excessive use of force, and racial bias in policing. The Act banned the use of 'no-knock' warrants in federal drug investigations and supported the states to adopt the same. Senator Rand Paul of Kentucky introduced the Breonna Taylor Act which prohibited federal law enforcement from carrying out a warrant until the officer can provide notice of his or her authority and purpose. The Louisville City Council adopted Breonna's Law which banned no-knock warrants and required officers to wear bodycams before, during, and after serving warrants.

In popular culture, the phrase 'Say Her Name' and the hashtag bearing the same referred to the call for justice in the killing of Breonna Taylor. When the halted 2019–2020 NBA season resumed, the Memphis Grizzlies wore t-shirts with Taylor's name and the hashtag on them as they entered the arena. The September 2020 edition of Oprah Winfrey's 'O' magazine featured Breonna Taylor's image on the cover, the only 'O' cover in the magazine's 20-year history that didn't bear Winfrey's image on the cover.

On 8 March 2023, the Department of Justice issued its report in a separate investigation into the Louisville Metro Police Department/Jefferson County Metro Government. The FBI found that the entities engaged in numerous policies and practices that violated the U.S. Constitution and federal law. The LMPD/JCMG consented to enter into an agreement working with an independent monitor to reform these practices. Some of the issues referenced included:

- excessive use of force, including the use of chokeholds, misuse of police dogs, and excessive use of Taser-type devices;
- searches conducted based upon invalid warrants, unlawful execution of warrants without knocking and announcing;
- unlawful stops, searches, detention, and arrests of persons during street enforcement operations;
- unlawfully discriminates against Black persons in its enforcement activities; and
- violating the rights of persons engaged in free speech against police brutality and critical of policing.

The report also indicates other deficiencies in the LMPD's response to persons with behavioral disorders and disabilities, investigations into domestic violence, and reports of officers involved in sexual misconduct or domestic violence. The DOJ report cites deficiencies in policy, training, supervision, and accountability that contributed to the issues within LMPD/JCMG.

Chapter 15
May 2020

On Memorial Day, 25 May 2020, while tensions were high following the shooting of Breonna Taylor, another event would occur which would result in massive protests, millions of dollars of damage, and propel the United States into a summer of protests, violence, and destruction. The torch would be lit in Minneapolis when George Floyd, a 44-year-old Black male was arrested by Minneapolis Police for allegedly passing a counterfeit $20 bill at a Minneapolis convenience store at about 8:00 pm. During the arrest, Floyd resisted, claimed breathing issues, claimed he suffered from claustrophobia, and pleaded with officers not to put him in the squad car.

At around 8:00 pm, Floyd had left the Cup Foods store in Minneapolis after purchasing cigarettes. Floyd was in his vehicle when store employees approached him and asked him to return the purchased items because the $20 bill that he had used to pay was counterfeit. Floyd refused to return the merchandise, so employees called Minneapolis Police and claimed Floyd had paid with 'fake' money, was drunk, and not in control of himself. Floyd was a regular customer at the store. A store security camera recorded the interaction between Floyd and the store employee.

At 8:08, Officers J. Alexander Kueng and Thomas Kieman Lane arrive on the scene and enter the Cup Foods store briefly then approach Floyd sitting in his SUV across the street in front of the Dragon Wok restaurant. Officer Lane tapped his flashlight on Floyd's vehicle window, startling him, and asked Floyd to show his hands. Floyd didn't comply so the officer repeated the request after tapping again. Floyd then apologized and opened the car door. Officer Lane repeated the show your hands request three more times. When Floyd didn't comply, Officer Lane drew his firearm, pointed it at Floyd's head, and demanded he show his hands. Floyd complied and the officer holstered the weapon. There was a brief struggle and Officer Lane pulled Floyd from the vehicle and handcuffed him. Floyd was placed in a seated position against the restaurant wall while the officer questioned the other occupants of the vehicle.

While Floyd was seated, Officer Lane asked him if 'he was on something' to which he responded, "No, nothing." Office Kueng told Floyd he was acting 'really erratic' and asked him about the foam around his mouth. Floyd responded that he had been 'hooping' earlier and that was why. 'Hooping' is slang for either playing basketball or using drugs, depending on the interpretation. Floyd then said he was calming down and remarked, "I'm feeling better now." At 8:13 pm, Officers Lane and Kueng told Floyd he was under arrest and walked him to the police car across the street. Floyd was leaning against the squad car door. Floyd said he was recovering from COVID-19, was claustrophobic, had anxiety, and that he didn't want to sit in the car. As officers attempted to place Floyd in the car, he repeatedly said, "I can't breathe," and begged them not to put him in the car, he even offered to lie on the ground instead.

A Minneapolis Park Police squad arrived, and that officer watched over Floyd's vehicle and the two occupants while the other officers were attempting to secure Floyd in their squad car. A third squad arrived with Officer Derek Chauvin and Tao Thao and Chauvin, the senior officer, assumed command of the encounter. Officer Chauvin asked if Floyd was being arrested and Officer Kueng replied he was arrested for forgery. Floyd and Officer Kueng were struggling in the backseat of the car for approximately one minute at this time.

Floyd said, "I can't f#@!ing breathe," twice during the struggle. Officer Chauvin then pulled Floyd across the vehicle's backseat from the driver's side to the passenger side and then Floyd exited the vehicle while police were pulling on him and he fell to the pavement.

Floyd was now lying on the pavement on the passenger side of the police vehicle with his head toward the rear of the vehicle. Floyd was lying face down and Officer Chauvin placed his left knee on the back of Floyd's neck and shoulder area, holding his head and upper body to the pavement. Officers Kueng, applied pressure to Floyd's torso region, and Lane, applied pressure to Floyd's legs and assisted Officer Chauvin in restraining the struggling and complaining Floyd on the pavement. During the time Floyd was being held to the ground, he repeatedly complained that his stomach hurt and he had difficulty breathing and asked the officers to please call for his mama. At one point, Officer Chauvin responded to Floyd by saying 'relax' after Floyd said, "I don't want to die."

A crowd of onlookers was standing on the sidewalk and began to advise the officers holding Floyd of his condition. Officer Thao positioned himself between the other officers and the bystanders to keep them on the sidewalk. One bystander said, "Look, he's bleeding from the nose." Another bystander said, "He's not resisting anymore. Just let him up." Another spoke to Floyd saying, "Just get in the car," and Floyd responded, "I can't." Officer Thao responded to one onlooker's comment with 'he's talking, he's fine'. He also makes a comment, "This is why you don't do drugs, kids."

After several minutes, Floyd appeared to fall unconscious. The onlookers urged the officers to check his pulse, roll him over, repeatedly saying that he was unconscious. Officer Kueng checked Floyd's wrist for a pulse but found none. Officers requested an ambulance for Floyd at this time but didn't change Floyd's position and continued to hold him on his stomach. Officer Lane asked Officer Chauvin if they should roll him over twice and Officer Chauvin responded with 'No'.

At 8:27 pm, an ambulance arrived, and medics checked Floyd's pulse and found none. Officers continued to hold Floyd in the stomach-down position for another minute until medics returned with a gurney and lifted Floyd onto the stretcher. After loading Floyd into the ambulance, Officer Lane entered the ambulance and checked Floyd's pulse. Floyd didn't have a pulse, so medics instructed Officer Lane to begin cardiopulmonary resuscitation (CPR). The ambulance then departed for the hospital. En route, medics requested additional assistance from the Minneapolis Fire Department which showed up at Cup Foods after the ambulance left the scene. The officers gave the Fire Department no information on Floyd's condition or the ambulance's whereabouts causing an additional delay in rendering necessary aid to Floyd. Floyd was pronounced dead at 9:27 pm at the hospital in Minneapolis.

The next day, 26 May, Minneapolis Police released a statement concerning Floyd's death. That statement indicated nothing about the tactics employed by the arresting officers used to control Floyd during the arrest, including Officer Chauvin's positioning his knee on Floyd's back and neck. The statement indicated that after Floyd exited his vehicle, he resisted arrest and officers were able to put him in handcuffs and that Floyd appeared to have suffered a medical emergency during the arrest process. Within hours of the statement's release, witnesses, security camera footage, and cell phone videos began appearing on the internet showing Floyd's arrest and his treatment at the hands of Minneapolis Police. The Minneapolis Police responded by updating their statement indicating 'new information' had 'been made available' and fired all four officers involved in Floyd's arrest and that the Federal Bureau of Investigation (FBI) had become involved in the investigation.

That same day, an autopsy was performed on George Floyd, and the cause of death was determined as cardiopulmonary arrest complicated by law enforcement subdual, restraint, and neck compression. The 1 June report indicates Floyd's condition was complicated by arteriosclerotic heart disease and hypertensive heart disease, including an enlarged heart and partial occlusion of multiple heart vessels. The report notes that fentanyl and methamphetamine usage may have increased the likelihood of death. The report also states Floyd had tested positive for SARS-COVID-19 on 3 April but does not assign that as a significant factor in the death.

A second autopsy commissioned by Floyd's family was performed which did not use toxicology results or tissue examination. That autopsy report released hours before the official autopsy by the county pathologist issued a different narrative, that Floyd's death was the result of asphyxia caused by compression of the neck and back, that Floyd died at the scene, and that Floyd had no pre-existing medical conditions which contributed to his death. That report also indicates that the ability to speak has no bearing on the ability to breathe.

In August, the autopsy conducted by the Hennepin County Pathologist was reviewed by the staff of the Office of the Armed Force Medical Examiner at the request of the Department of Justice (DOJ). The reviewers concluded that the county autopsy was more credible and reported that the police 'subdual and restraint had elements of positional and mechanical asphyxiation'.

On 29 May 2020, former Officer Derek Chauvin was arrested for third-degree murder in the death of George Floyd. On 3 June, Chauvin's charges were upgraded to second-degree murder, and the other officers were charged in the death of George Floyd with aiding and abetting Chauvin as well as lesser charges that were added. Beyond the criminal charges, multiple investigations by state entities and federal offices were opened in early June. The DOJ opened investigations into the Minneapolis Police Department and whether federal civil rights violations had been committed by the officers themselves.

The investigations into the Minneapolis Police Department would conclude in 2022 and 2023. The results would indicate that the Minneapolis Police Department had systemic problems, including racial bias in policing, excessive use of force, deficient training standards and practices, and a general paramilitary culture with a lack of accountability, among other issues.

Chauvin and the other officers were found guilty of state charges and federal civil rights violations during their trials. Chauvin was sentenced to 22.5 years in prison on State charges and 21 years in the federal case. The other officers received sentences ranging from 3 years to 4.5 years on State charges and 2.5 years to 3.5 years in their federal cases. Floyd's family filed a wrongful death lawsuit against the Minneapolis Police Department and settled that claim for $27 million in 2021. The settlement eclipsed the $20 million record previously settled by Minneapolis in 2019 for the wrongful death of Justine Damond. Ms. Damond was an Australian tourist who was killed by Minneapolis Police Officer Muhammed Noor in a shooting incident. Officer Noor was also convicted of murder charges following that incident.

As with other deaths, protests and demonstrations against police excessive use of force and racial bias occurred. On 26 May, the first protest was organized in Minneapolis. Within a number of days, protests and demonstrations had spread across the U.S. and into 60 countries around the world. Over 2,000 U.S. cities were affected by these protests.

Although many of the protests were peaceful, some turned violent and destructive. In Minneapolis, a protest that started peacefully turned destructive as acts of vandalism took place. At the 3rd Precinct of the Minneapolis Police Department, protestors broke windows, tore down fences, and broke into the front entrance of the building. Police retreated to the roof and fired tear gas and less-than-lethal rounds at protestors while staff evacuated the building. The protestors started fires in the building and the building was burned to the ground. Nearby, a 200-unit apartment building under construction was also destroyed in acts of arson. Police responded with riot gear, rubber bullets, tear gas, and flash grenades but the rioters pressed ahead throwing rocks and objects at the police. Over the next several days, as night fell in Minneapolis, riots erupted. In total, over 1,500 businesses in Minneapolis and nearby St. Paul were damaged, looted, or destroyed. In total, 67 buildings were destroyed by fires set by the rioters. The City of Minneapolis had initiated a curfew which did nothing to stop the demonstrations. The Minnesota Governor activated 500

National Guard troops and even this was insufficient to stop the mass demonstrations. By the time it was over, 18 persons had been killed in the violence and over $350 million in property damage had been done in Minneapolis.

The destructive and violent protests were not limited to the Minneapolis area. Protestors calling for justice for George Floyd and rallying against police brutality caused 12 major U.S. cities to impose curfews. Twelve states called upon National Guard troops to try to curtail the growing demonstrations. Three weeks after George Floyd's death, the demonstrations and protests now represented a new movement, 'Defund the Police'. This movement represented efforts to reform and in some cases, eliminate, police departments in cities and states. The calls, supported and promoted by the Black Lives Matter organization, reached deep into political races and corporate America. Corporations and professional sports teams and their associated leagues donated large sums of money to the Black Lives Matter groups to show their support. The fields and stadiums were decorated with slogans and banners, the uniforms were adorned with slogans and symbols.

U.S. city leaders and politicians echoed and seized upon the movement to further their ambitions. Many U.S. cities, including Washington, D.C. and New York City had 'Black Lives Matter' painted on city streets in avenue-wide letters. Many cities considered major adjustments to their police budgets and leadership. Huge budget reductions and cancelations of specialty units were enacted in many cities.

In Seattle, Washington, protestors and rioters laid siege and barricaded off a major portion of the Seattle downtown area. Within the so-called 'CHOP' (Capitol Hill Occupied Protest) or 'CHAZ' (Capitol Hill Autonomous Zone), no police or emergency personnel were allowed. Armed persons monitored and patrolled the perimeter. Residents and business owners were not allowed into their homes or businesses within the zone under the protestors' control. Seattle Mayor Jenny Durkan referred to the protests and demonstrations as maybe another 'Summer of Love' in an interview with CNN's Chris Cuomo. Whether she was referring to the 1967 riots and demonstrations or to 'Woodstock' is uncertain. What is sure, is that within the area, shootings and even one death would occur, as well as attempted arson, and multiple reports of sexual assaults. Even after these events, Mayor Durkan restated that she believed the city could work out a peaceful solution with the 'occupiers' to provide an environment for continued peaceful protest.

In Portland, Oregon, protestors and rioters surrounded the Multnomah County Justice Center on 29 May. An initially peaceful vigil turned into a riot when protestors entered the building and set fires throughout while corrections department records workers were still inside. The rioters then fanned out across the city and started vandalizing and looting. After these events, the City of Portland enacted, then abandoned an 8:00 pm curfew. The Portland Police Chief resigned after criticism that the department wasn't diverse enough. A U.S. District Court Judge issued a temporary restraining order against the police using tear gas and other crowd control measures. Then the Portland City Council voted to reduce the Portland Police Departments (PPD) budget by $15 million. These victories only encouraged the protestors to continue their efforts and renew their demands for a $50 million cut to the PPD.

The protestors turned their attention to the U.S. District Court building in July and this brought federal police services into the fray. Crowds of protestors clashed with federal officers nightly. The protestors fired commercial-grade fireworks at the officers and used lasers to shine into the officers' eyes. The protestors also used frozen water bottles, bricks, rocks, and other projectiles against the officers. The federal officers responded with tear gas, rubber bullets, arrests and detentions, and other less-than-lethal means available to them.

By the end of July, the Oregon governor replaced the federal officers with the Oregon State Police. In mid-August, the Oregon State Police withdrew entirely after the newly elected district attorney announced he wouldn't prosecute any demonstrators who had been arrested. The protestors saw this as another victory and continued their efforts. In late August, during a pro-Trump caravan, a man associated with a prayer group was killed after he was confronted by two men associated with the protests. The man who shot him identified himself as a '100% ANTIFA' member in his social media posts and said the man's death was part of 'warfare'. The shooter was shot and killed by federal agents when they attempted to arrest him several days later.

Across the United States, statues and memorials were disfigured, destroyed, or torn down. Statues of Abraham Lincoln, Thomas Jefferson, Civil War Generals, and other major U.S. figures of historical importance were assaulted. Cities removed statues and placed them in storage during the middle of the night, removing them before they could be targeted by protests. The civil unrest continued throughout the summer and into the fall which led to a presidential election. The political rhetoric and divisions combined with COVID-19 fears, lockdowns, and restrictions intended to curb the spread of the disease only served to increase the unrest. By the end of the summer, over $2 billion of damage had been done across the United States by demonstrations and protests and 25 lives had been lost because of those events.

Chapter 16
Cultural Influences and Police Practices Reviewed

Over the past several chapters, we have reviewed some of the more well-known cases that have influenced our culture and formed social opinions about law enforcement and racial bias-related issues. The cases included are not the only cases that involved claims of excessive use of force by police and racially biased policing policies and procedures, or governmental practices which targeted racial minorities.

The phrase 'Say Their Names' can be seen on protest signs, t-shirts, and other materials including social media postings and sites. The 'Say Their Names' campaign was developed by the African American Policy Forum as an effort to bring awareness to the cases of persons who were victims of police excessive use of force. The campaign also uses the phrase as a memorial slogan, so that the names of these persons are not forgotten over time. The list of names is ongoing and the fact that their cases weren't presented herein is not meant to suggest they are any less important or influential in the social and cultural changes that have occurred or may occur.

The cases presented in the previous chapters each, or together, highlight a specific characteristic of law enforcement activity that resulted in the death of someone important. The fact that those cases were high profile, also meant researching them and obtaining information about them was readily available. It was imperative that the cases being retold herein were presented in a fact-based manner to reduce bias, innuendo, and erroneous information which has persisted in the social and cultural narrative. If we, as a society, are to move past the division into reasonable reforms and a new era of law enforcement, we must work from facts, not emotions and agendas.

The case of Trayvon Martin was not a law enforcement-involved case per se but involved a codified right to self-defense under Florida law. The same doctrine that the Florida Legislature had adopted into state law was being used, in whole or in part, in 37 other states to define the self-defense laws. George Zimmerman relied upon the laws of the State of Florida which were duly enacted to defend himself against the legal ramifications of his actions that night. That distinction must be made clear, the law specified what was considered justifiable.

The actions of Trayvon Martin and George Zimmerman that fateful day set them on a course that ultimately would lead to one of their deaths. The events leading up to their altercation, if handled differently by one party or the other, or by both, would have ultimately changed the outcome, possibly. We will never know because we cannot go back and change the choices of either at the time. Similarly, the choices of actions made by the witnesses, investigators, prosecuting attorneys, and others involved in the legal process affected the outcome of the case, in compliance with the law.

The effect of Trayvon Martin's death on the social fabric of our society was also important. Because the initial investigating police department made the determination that they couldn't disprove Zimmerman's claims of self-defense, there were no initial charges filed in Martin's death. Martin's family enlisted the service of a civil rights attorney who used the internet and social media to create pressure on Florida governmental officials to investigate and bring charges. The attorney also turned to African American community leaders such as Jesse Jackson and Al Sharpton to generate nationwide interest in the case. NBA stars like Lebron James, Carmelo Anthony, and Amari Stoudemire and their teammates joined the campaign to pressure for legal action. Even President Obama commented on the case, increasing the exposure. The Florida governor was pressured into appointing a Special Investigator who brought criminal charges against Zimmerman without empaneling a Grand Jury to consider legal charges. This could have resulted in Zimmerman being denied his rights under the Fifth Amendment.

After Zimmerman was acquitted in a jury trial, protests and demonstrations followed. One person commenting on Facebook wrote three simple words on her post, 'Black lives matter.' That phrase would be picked up and turned into a movement against police excessive use of force and racial injustice.

In New York, Eric Garner uttered the words, 'I Can't Breathe' 11 times during his encounter with New York Police officers. Garner, a 6-foot 2-inch, 400-pound man was told by police officers that he was being arrested for illegally selling 'loosies' (single cigarettes). During the conversation, Garner told the officers he didn't do anything and wasn't going to cooperate with them this time. An officer, standing behind Garner attempted to handcuff Garner by grabbing his right arm near the wrist and extending the arm to bring it behind Garner's back. This move is referred to as an arm-bar hold and is commonly used by police during handcuffing processes. Garner spun into the move and defeated the maneuver, so the officer transitioned into what is referred to as a 'rear takedown' or 'seatbelt' maneuver. Garner was significantly taller and larger than the officer so Garner again defeated this move by raising his arms and pushing backward. This caused both Garner and the officer to fall to the sidewalk.

Garner was handcuffed with the assistance of several additional officers while he was lying on the ground, face down. Garner was transported to a hospital several minutes later as he complained of medical distress. Garner died of cardiac arrest about an hour later. During his transport to the hospital, Garner apparently suffered a heart attack. The coroner's report would say Garner's death was the result of complications caused by the application of a chokehold by the officer. The coroner's report including the inflammatory language of a 'chokehold' would create a firestorm of controversy.

This case is all about control techniques used by police officers during the arrest process and about post-arrest care and positioning. Police officers are taught many different techniques that are non-lethal and intended to aid them in subduing a non-compliant resisting subject. This allows the officer to handcuff and neutralize a subject's ability to resist and cause harm to the officer or others. With the growth of mixed martial arts training for both fitness and fighting skills, officers are also being taught these skills. Not only to employ but also to counter possible attacks against them. Although these techniques do result in pain or discomfort, they are considered non-lethal force when properly used. Another important aspect of the arrest process is the post-arrest positioning of the subject. Once a person is subdued and under control, the person should be placed in a position where they can be controlled, monitored, and in a safe location.

After Garner's death, the New York Police Department Commissioner ordered a review of NYPD training programs involving the use of force during detention and arrest, including restraint or control holds. The New York State Assemblies overwhelmingly passed the Eric Garner Anti-Chokehold Act which imposes criminal sentences on police officers who use any form of possible chokehold upon a person.

Following the investigation into Garner's death, a Grand Jury was presented with the evidence and testimony related to the case. After deliberations, the Grand Jury decided not to indict the officer involved in the struggle with Garner during the arrest. A federal investigation by the Department of Justice also found that the officer was compliant with the training and practices of the NYPD during the arrest. Concluding that the struggle causing Garner and the officer to fall to the sidewalk is what caused the officer's hand to move to Garner's neck. That position lasted a total of seven seconds during the arrest process. The report also indicated the size disparity between Garner and the officer contributed to the improper positioning of the officer's arm and hand during the attempted control hold.

The protests and demonstrations that followed Garner's death spread across the United States. The phrase 'I Can't Breathe' became a slogan in the struggle for racial justice and against police excessive force. Sports stars in the NBA, the NFL, and some NCAA basketball teams supported the effort by displaying the slogan. Other influential persons in music and art incorporated 'I Can't Breathe' into their art and lyrics. In New York, after the Grand Jury announcement of no indictments, one person took matters into his own hands, ambushing and killing two NYPD officers while they sat in their vehicle. The assassin then killed himself, denying justice for the slain officers.

In Ferguson, Missouri, Michael Brown and his friend were walking down the middle of a city street when an officer of the Ferguson Police Department passed them and advised them to use the sidewalk. This simple exchange would be the catalyst for an encounter that would ultimately lead to Michael Brown's death. Michael Brown's response to the officer by cursing at him would cause the officer to initiate a further encounter with the two men. In terms of a law enforcement activity, this is called a causal encounter or public safety encounter. Although I can't speak to why the officer advised the two men to move to the sidewalk, I can guess it was simply for their safety and to ensure the regular flow of traffic.

Based on the investigation reports, it didn't appear as if the officer had any other intent. There were witnesses who were driving on the same roadway, so the initial advisement seemed to be normal and reasonable. It was only after Brown reacted to the officer's direction that the officer initiated a direct encounter with the two men. The officer positioned his vehicle to block their path and directed them to come over to him and that is when this encounter went upside down. For some reason, Michael Brown acted to assault the officer. The officer fought back, using force to protect himself from the assault. When Brown fled, the officer pursued and when Brown stopped and charged, the officer used force to stop the assaulting Brown.

The social impact of this incident came when the companion, who wasn't identified or interviewed after the event, spoke to the media. His story, later proved by forensic science and admitted by him to be falsified, became the story. In his interviews with the media, he stated that Michael Brown had been shot by the officer, execution-like, after he had surrendered and had his hands up and said, "Don't shoot." The phrase 'Hand's Up, Don't Shoot' became another slogan embodying the racial injustice against minorities and the excessive use of force by police against them.

The facts of the Michael Brown shooting only came out after extensive investigation. The investigations took months, but the reaction was intense and immediate. The reaction led to violent protests, countered by more force from the police. The police reaction was again seen as overly aggressive, and the governor had to direct state police to tone down the demonstrations. Unfortunately, the city of Ferguson would be destroyed in the process of restoring order.

The real tragedy in this incident would be that the patterns and practices of the city of Ferguson, The Ferguson Police Department, and the St. Louis County Court system would not receive the attention they deserved from the public. The investigations would discover that they all employed serious racial biases including targeted over-policing of minority citizens, policies of financial disparate treatment in the courts, and policies of 'quotas' for police performance evaluations and advancement. These practices created the environment in which Brown lived and possibly how he envisioned the police and the legal system. Brown and the officer would collide in this atmosphere, and the result would be tragic.

In Baltimore, the case of Freddie Gray would bring scrutiny upon two more activities of law enforcement, saturation enforcement (or enhanced patrol) and in-custody transport. During targeted enforcement activities, Baltimore police officers using bicycles would be patrolling an area near the Gilmor Homes housing project. This area had been identified for enhanced enforcement activities due to high-crime activity. The officers were noticed by Freddie Gray and Gray would flee from them. The officers chased Gray and after stopping him conducted a frisk for weapons. The officers arrested him after finding what they identified as a spring-assisted knife, a switchblade, on his person. Because the officers were using bicycles, they called for a transport van, a 'paddy-wagon', to transport Gray to Central Processing for detention. The enhanced enforcement effort was not targeted at any specific criminal activity. The purpose was to get people engaged in criminal activity of any kind, off the streets and into the court process.

Once the transport vehicle arrived, Gray started resisting the officers' efforts to load him into the back of the vehicle. Gray's yelling and antics attracted a crowd of onlookers who started yelling at the officers and supporting Gray. Gray continued to resist by alternately kicking his legs and 'going limp' and refusing to assist in walking or supporting himself during the loading process. The officers eventually loaded Gray into the back of the transport van and then loud banging and yelling could be heard from inside the vehicle. Gray was the only person in the back of the vehicle.

As the driver was enroute to Central Processing, he called for an officer to meet him near an intersection. The driver and another officer met, and that officer spoke to Gray and helped him to sit up on the bench of the van. After the conversation, it was determined that Gray needed to be cleared medically before he could be processed into the central booking area, so a plan was made to take him for medical evaluation. At about this time, another call for transport assistance was received so the van responded to that location to secure another subject for transport. Gray was checked at that time and still requested medical attention.

Once the vehicle left that location en route to drop the second subject off at a nearby station, the other subject reported he heard loud banging on the center dividing wall, like someone banging their head on the metal wall. Upon arrival at the station, Gray was found unconscious lying on the floor of the transport vehicle with froth along his mouth. Medics were called to provide aid and transport Gray to the hospital. After a week and significant efforts, including surgery, Gray died a week later from complications related to the surgical attempts to repair his fractured spine.

There were no cameras in the transport vehicle to record what happened to Gray. According to the other transport subject, the ride was unremarkable with no sudden stops, starts, or aggressive turns. Gray was not seat-belted to the bench as required by the new Baltimore Police Department policy which had gone into effect six days earlier. The only thing that could be certain was that Gray was injured during the transport process while in the custody of the Baltimore Police.

Once again, a city would be thrown into chaos and destroyed by looting, arson, and violent demonstrations citing police brutality. Social media had spread the videos from Gray's initial arrest and the second stop where he was secured in shackles. These formed the narrative that Gray was mistreated during his arrest which led to his injuries. The riots and demonstrations would serve as cover for what appeared to be the systematic targeting of Asian and Arab-owned businesses in Baltimore. Another target of looting would be pharmacies and methadone clinics in Baltimore, probably for the drugs that they had inside them. Those drugs would fuel an explosion of black-market drug sales in the city for months.

After almost three weeks of demonstrations, looting, arson, and rioting, the city began to settle down. The National Guard, which had been activated by the Maryland Governor, to perform security and enforce a curfew in the city began to deactivate and leave. The protestors in Baltimore had complained of overly aggressive policing and tactics. Following the events that had transpired, the citizens of Baltimore would get less policing. By the end of the year, arrests had dropped by 50% in Baltimore, shooting incidents had increased greatly, and the number of homicides jumped. One officer commented after the disturbances had ended, we (the police) felt unsupported by the government leaders and our management. He continued, the people of Baltimore seemed to want less policing, that's what they're getting.

Just after the 4 July holiday in 2016, two cases involving armed encounters between citizens and police occurred, resulting in the deaths of both citizens. The events would occur on back-to-back days and happen across the country from each other, but their combined effect would be important in affecting change. In Louisiana, Alton Sterling was approached by police after a report that he had threatened someone with a pistol outside a local store. In Minnesota, the following day, Philando Castile, driving his vehicle, was stopped in an area where a robbery had occurred because the officer believed he matched the description of a suspect in that crime. Both Sterling and Castile would be shot by police officers within less than 90 seconds after the initiation of the encounter.

In the case of Alton Sterling, officers were called to the location knowing that a subject had displayed a gun. Their knowledge may have put them in a certain frame of mind upon arrival. The officer who initiated the contact with Sterling approached him quickly and directly, issuing him orders immediately. There was no explanation given by the officer as to why they were ordering him to do things. Sterling responded as may be expected, with confusion and asking questions. This caused the officers to escalate their use of force as Sterling was resisting by failing to follow their commands, even though Sterling didn't know why. Sterling responded by escalating his resistance which led to the officers using a less-than-lethal device, an electronic control device or Taser, which only momentarily disabled Sterling. After the initial deployment of the Taser, Sterling and an officer, engaged in a hand-to-hand fight on the ground. The officer's pre-knowledge that Sterling had a gun in his pocket caused him to attempt to control Sterling's arm but when he was unable to do that, he used deadly force and shot Sterling multiple times, killing him. The whole encounter was over in less than 90 seconds.

This did not have to happen. The officer's initial approach to Sterling could have been completely different. With the glorious ability to review this matter after the fact and critique each person's actions and reactions, we can come up with a completely different result. Our ability to role-play the different actions and reactions allows us that luxury. Unfortunately, that is not how law enforcement works. Things tend to happen very rapidly and there is little time to step back and change the direction of an encounter as it happens. As commonly used in military jargon, every plan is perfect right up until the first action, or shot is taken. Then everything is up in the air.

In the case of Philando Castile, we have a little different fact situation but again we have an encounter between a police officer and a person who has a gun on their person. Castile was driving along a city street returning from grocery shopping with his girlfriend and her four-year-old daughter. A police officer patrolling in the area saw the vehicle and occupants and reported to another officer that he thought the driver matched the description of a recent robbery suspect in the area. The officer intended to pull over the vehicle and identify the subjects inside. The officer waited to stop the vehicle until another officer was available to assist him during the stop.

When the officer initiated the stop on Castile's vehicle, the driver stopped immediately. The officer approached the driver's window, and the backup officer approached the passenger door of the vehicle. The officer asked Castile for his driver's license and vehicle information and Castile handed the officer his insurance information. Castile told the officer he had a pistol on his person. He told the officer he was getting his driver's license and started to retrieve his wallet from his pocket. Initially, the officer nonchalantly responded to Castile's statement about his pistol by saying, "Okay, don't pull it out." After several seconds, the officer reacted to Castile's statement and his movements more aggressively stating don't go for it or something to that effect. Castile and the front seat passenger both responded he was not pulling it out. The officer continued to repeat his commands and with Castile's continued movement, the officer drew his weapon and fired several shots into Castile.

Castile slumped forward leaning onto the steering wheel and moaned, "I wasn't going for it." His girlfriend in the front seat exclaimed, "You just killed my boyfriend," and used her cell phone to broadcast the event using a new publicly available application, Facebook Live©.

As Castile was bleeding to death from the gunshot wounds, his death was broadcast across the internet. The entire interaction between the officer and Castile lasted 45 seconds. The officer claimed he thought Castile was reaching for the weapon when he shot him to defend himself.

Both cases involved armed encounters between law enforcement and the public. In one case, the suspect had reportedly threatened another person with the weapon prompting the call to the police. In the other, the armed person was legally permitted to carry the weapon and made no threats or displays of the weapon. He promptly informed the officer that he had the weapon. In both cases, the officers appeared to have escalated to deadly force very quickly. Although the officers may have been legally justified in their actions and didn't face criminal trial, they were both fired from their employment and the departments paid large wrongful death settlements to the victims' families.

In early 2020, Breonna Taylor was killed when she was struck by rounds fired by a Louisville Metro Police Department (LMPD) officer while that officer and his partners were serving a 'no-knock' warrant. That type of warrant, granted in special circumstances where police investigators claim that danger will exist and can be magnified if persons know that police are present is supposed to be the exception, not a common thing. In this case, the warrant was being served in a potential drug-related case on the apartment of Breonna Taylor at 12:40 am by members of a drug task force operated by LMPD. The task force members had not obtained the warrant or developed the information for the warrant, they were simply the officers assigned to execute the warrant. The investigators who prepared and presented the information to a judge to obtain the warrant were not present during the service. The service of 'no-knock' warrants, the development of the information supporting the issuance of the warrant, and the officer's behavior were all issues in this tragic case.

Because the officers were advised of some information prior to the service of the warrant, they did knock and announce their presence prior to entering the apartment. Witnesses to the incident reported they were alerted to the police activity by the officers knocking and announcing. During post-incident interviewing, Taylor's boyfriend, Kenneth Walker, said that Ms. Taylor had commented something to the effect of who was at the door, possibly.

The fact that nobody opened the door caused the officers to use a battering ram to break open the door. When the first officer entered the apartment, Kenneth Walker fired at the officer and struck him in the leg, causing that officer to fall into the entryway. The other officers returned fire into the apartment in response to the shots fired at them. One officer fired from the doorway and another officer moved outside the building and fired into the apartment through a glass patio door and window. Both the patio door and the window were covered with blackout fabric and blinds which prevented that officer from seeing where his rounds were going.

Although Walker was unhurt in the exchange of gunfire, Ms. Taylor was struck several times and died of her wounds at the scene. After the shootings, Walker was arrested for shooting the officer. The apartment was never searched for the supposed drug activity or proceeds as indicated in the warrant. The rounds fired by the officer that fired through the window and patio door passed into neighboring apartments, endangering those residents as well.

Post-incident investigations revealed several things not only with the officer's behaviors but also with the practices of the LMPD and the Jefferson County Metro Government (JCMG). The investigators who had presented the information to a judge to obtain the warrant had used old or erroneous information as a basis for the warrant. When Breonna Taylor was killed during the service of the warrant, those investigators created fictitious records to support the information they presented to the judge to try to cover their mistakes or malpractice. This information was discovered during investigations following Breonna Taylor's death and those investigators are facing state and federal charges for those actions.

The officer who fired into the apartment through the window and patio door, without being able to see what was beyond was terminated for use of force policy violations. This officer's actions violated one of the first rules of firearm safety, always know the direction of the muzzle and what is beyond it. This is a very basic rule of firearm safety that every person who has received some training in firearm handling, be they a hunter, firearm-carrying citizen, or trained police officer should know. The officer also was charged with wanton endangerment under state law for endangering the persons in the neighboring apartments. The officer was charged with federal civil rights violations as well.

The issue of the use of 'no-knock' warrants not only affected the LMPD but also was reviewed nationwide. Following Breonna Taylor's death, LMPD banned the issuance and service of these warrants. LMPD also implemented a policy that all officers serving warrants would activate and wear body cameras five minutes before, during, and at least five minutes after a warrant is served. In the case of Breonna Taylor's death, none of the officers were wearing body cams at the time of the service of the warrant. Many municipalities across the country also stopped the service of 'no-knock' warrants in their jurisdictions as well.

Public protests and demonstrations following Breonna Taylor's death were subdued because of the COVID-19 outbreak. Many cities had strict lockdowns and restrictions on large gatherings of the public which prohibited organized events such as sporting events, concerts, and permitted demonstrations. The lack of demonstrations did not reduce the racial tensions that had developed concerning police excessive use of force. Legislative efforts were introduced at the state of federal levels named in honor of Breonna Taylor which enacted reforms concerning warrant service by law enforcement.

Within several weeks of Breonna Taylor's death, the death of George Floyd would occur, and that event would result in massive protests, demonstrations, and destruction of property. The case of George Floyd in Minneapolis was not only an excessive use of force case, but it was also a display of utter disregard for a person's well-being and life. While Officer Chauvin knelt on Mr. Floyd's neck holding him semi-face down on the street, other officers failed to act to protect Mr. Floyd from the physical assault. While bystanders watched, yelled at the officers to help Floyd, and recorded the events, Mr. Floyd slowly lost consciousness and died from a condition called positional asphyxiation. Floyd being held in this position restricted his ability to breathe resulting in his losing consciousness. Even after Floyd lost consciousness, the officers took no action to alleviate Floyd's distress or address his medical needs. Even after medical technicians arrived, the officers did not reposition Floyd to assist his medical condition. Floyd had pre-existing conditions that were aggravated by his treatment which contributed to his death, but this doesn't absolve the officers of their treatment of George Floyd.

Most law enforcement officers are trained in basic first aid and receive training in medical emergencies. One such basic skill is the response to choking incidents. During a choking incident, it is commonly taught that if a person can speak, wheeze, cough, or otherwise make noise, the responder shouldn't do anything other than stand by and be ready to assist the person. This is because a person cannot do any of those things without moving air into and out of their lungs. This medical responder training is usually conducted on an annual basis for officers. With this training, an officer's first response when someone complains they cannot breathe is based upon this training. During George Floyd's arrest, an onlooker tells Officer Tao that Floyd isn't breathing. Officer Tao responds with 'he's talking, he's fine', dismissing the reported lack of breathing observations of the bystander. The officer was relying on his training and not using rational thinking during the situation.

George Floyd's death would ignite a fury of demonstrations and violent protests which would continue well into the summer. Protests against police excessive use of force would sweep across the U.S. and morph into a summer of discontent, resulting in prolonged violent confrontations in many cities. The rise of the Black Lives Matter movement would result in corporate support of efforts against abuses by police against minorities. These protests would spread to many other countries. Combined with COVID-19 restrictions and lockdowns, an upcoming contentious presidential election, and multiple triggering incidents of police use of force, the United States would be thrown into chaos by the demonstrations. A display not witnessed in the United States since the Vietnam era anti-war and Civil Rights movements of the 1960s and early 1970s.

A new call would rise through the voices of protest, 'Defund the Police.' These calls would affect the budgets of police departments in many major cities across the country, resulting in major funding cuts. The 'Defund the Police' movement would result in a significant loss of support by government members of police officers and their work. Combining the loss of support, the loss of funding, and the loss of purpose, police officers would start leaving the job.

Chapter 17
A Nation Divided

When a relatively unknown Abraham Lincoln was campaigning for the position of United States Senator for the State of Illinois against Stephen A. Douglas in 1858, the nation had already been struggling with the issue of slavery. The country was expanding and at issue was the extension of slavery into the newly recognized states. The issue was ever-present, but no one wanted to talk openly about what may happen. Everyone knew that slavery was a divisive and determining issue and that something had to be definitively resolved, but nobody wanted to be the one to fan the embers that were smoldering and ignite the fire.

Lincoln had won the nomination of the Republican Party to run against the incumbent Democrat Senator Douglas. The Democrat Party was pro-slavery yet Douglas was considered a moderate by Republicans, who were anti-slavery. The Republicans thought they could work a compromise regarding the issue with the Democrat Douglas. During the campaign, Lincoln and Douglas engaged in several debates, where each candidate presented their views on issues through the delivery of short speeches.

Douglas believed that new states should determine the legality of slavery in that state through popular sovereignty, where the people of the state decided to be economically slave or free. He believed if the people were to exercise their own destiny, the angst between slave and free states would naturally dimmish, resulting in a return to peaceful co-existence.

Lincoln on the other hand believed that the Dred Scott v. Sandford ruling of the United States Supreme Court a year prior, in 1857, had made that point moot. Dred Scott and his wife, both enslaved persons, were brought to a non-slave territory by their enslaver, a military surgeon and officer, and Scott attempted to sue in court to establish his status as a freeman. The Supreme

Court ruled that the Amendments to the Constitution did not grant citizenship to African Americans, whether free or slave, and therefore they [Africans] did not possess the right to sue in federal court and deserved no federal protections in court. For Lincoln, the natural extension of this ruling was the right to vote. The Dred Scott decision is still considered one of the most heinous decisions ever made by the Supreme Court. Remember, the Fourteenth Amendment, which was adopted after the civil war, made African Americans citizens of the United States.

Lincoln's speech during a debate on 16 June became one of his most well-known speeches, even if it essentially ended his Senate campaign. In the speech, Lincoln drew from the Bible and the books of Mark, Chapter 3, verse 25 and Matthew, Chapter 12, verse 25 where Jesus speaks of a divided house to His Disciples. Lincoln's words were:

"A house divided against itself, cannot stand. I believe this government cannot endure permanently half slave and half free. I do not expect the Union to be dissolved—I do not expect the house to fall—but I do expect it will cease to be divided. It will become all one thing or all the other. Either the opponents of slavery will arrest the further spread of it, and place it where the public mind shall rest in the belief that it is in the course of ultimate extinction; or it's advocates will push it forward, till it shall become lawful in all the States, old as well as new—North as well as South."

Lincoln's intentions were to draw a distinction between himself and Douglas' opinions, it was not to draw the country into civil war. He was simply trying to say if the people allow slavery to persist in the Southern states legally, and to expand as desired into new states, there will always be slavery and it will infect even the non-slave states. The recent Dred Scott decision would permit slave holders to resettle in non-slave states and bring slavery with them, essentially converting those states to slave states. Lincoln's words were intended to be prophetic to the public, warning of where the expansion of slavery would bring the country.

Lincoln's words were used against him during the rest of the Senate campaign by Douglas making Lincoln out to be a proponent for civil war. The speech was portrayed as a call to conflict to resolve the issue of slavery, one way or the other, once and for all. Lincoln lost the Illinois Senate election, but his words energized a fledgling Republican Party and brought him national notoriety. Two years later, Lincoln would win the Republican ticket nomination for president. After his presidential election, his prophetic words would come to be as the Southern slave states decided to secede from the Union. The civil war would begin in 1861 as Lincoln attempted to hold the Union together. Eighteen months later, Lincoln would deliver the Emancipation Proclamation, changing the meaning of the war from maintaining the Union to abolishing slavery.

Today, the country seems as divided over many issues as it was back in the 1850s over the issue of slavery. Whether abortion is legal or not nationwide. The Supreme Court has ruled that the issue rests with the states to determine, just as was proposed over slavery. The political divisions between Democrats and Republicans, seem to widen each election cycle, and neither seems to be able to compromise over any issue. Hardliners on both sides push those with moderate viewpoints to bend to their will. The vocal minority is driving the silent majority to accommodate them or face a backlash of retribution and possible cancelation or 'blacklisting'. The country struggles to determine what to do about immigration, who should be allowed in, and how they should be admitted. There is great division over the education of children. Some advocate that the schools, not the parents, should determine what is right for children to learn, and what is not. Some even propose to educate the children using revisionist views of history. Should we teach children that the Holocaust inflicted upon the Jewish people by the National Socialist (Nazi) Party of Germany did not happen and is just fiction? That during World War II, the Japanese military authority did not murder hundreds of thousands and possibly millions of Chinese, Korean, Vietnamese, Filipino, and other Asian peoples as they were thought to be lesser subvariants of humans? What about age-appropriate education regarding sex, sexual orientation, and other personal choices? How about the rights of parents to be informed and involved in the decisions of their children over what could be life-changing medical or personal decisions?

All of those topics could be their own chapter, but this book is about law enforcement and how culture determines the course of the law, and its enforcement by and for the people.

Our culture is undergoing major changes related to policing, privacy, and personal beliefs. In some ways, the nation has gradually moved away from

Judeo-Christian values of family, faith, and country. Less than 50% of the country's population regularly attends religious services. Some equate the reduction in religious service attendance to reductions in moral values and the bond of family units.

Law enforcement in the United States is undergoing these same cultural changes, as well as adapting to other cultural changes. The cases presented in the previous chapters highlighted many of the issues with traditional law enforcement in the United States. For many decades, law enforcement has operated in an environment where the members of the group enforced the code of conduct upon the other members. What was right was right, if something was wrong, little or nothing was said to correct it. This mentality was reinforced through the training of new officers in the field by officers who had grown up and lived by that code of conduct. The common training mantra was, forget what you learned at the academy, the street is where the real learning happens. Training practices and programs should be updated, and training officers should be evaluated regularly as to what, and how, they are training new officers. Officer Chauvin was training new officers at the time he knelt on and killed George Floyd. Should he have been training new officers in his method of exerting control over a person?

Some of this conduct has persisted for many decades and harkens back to a racially divided country prior to the civil rights movement. Racially divisive policies and practices persist in government, courts, and law enforcement, and must be exposed and eradicated. Still more onerous is the unequal application of law by our courts and by our criminal justice system. The criminal justice system is just that, a system. When one component, be it the police, the investigators, the prosecutors, or the courts, does not execute their responsibilities equally and justly, the system fails. In the case of the Ferguson Police Department and the St. Louis County Court system, the practices and policies reinforced the unequal application of law upon the mostly minority community members. These practices led to racial tension which may have contributed to Michael Brown's reactions and ultimately his death.

Our criminal justice system is depicted in art and symbolism as the Lady of Justice, blindfolded, carrying scales to weigh harm caused versus justice delivered, and wielding a sword, used to dispense justice as needed. The Lady of Justice is blindfolded so as not to be swayed by the physical, considering only information and facts provided using the scales to judge the competing interests.

Our notion of justice is not new, the Egyptian society some 4,000 years ago depicted something similar in their pyramid art. The Egyptian god Maat, later to become Isis, was depicted with a scale weighing a person's heart in death to determine their worth and whether they could pass into the afterlife. To pass into the afterlife, a person's heart was expected to weigh less than a feather, meaning it carried nothing with it to burden the soul in the afterlife. For the living, Maat's scales were used to balance issues of justice and settle disputes between persons.

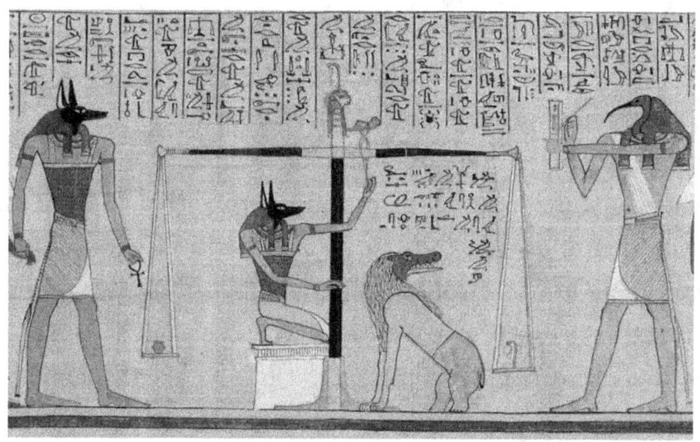

Egyptian God Maat weighing the heart of Hunefer against a feather.
https://en.wikipedia.org/wiki/File:El_pesado_del_coraz%C3%B3n_en_el_Papiro_de_Hunefer
.jpg

Our criminal justice system is critical to the functionality of our government and our society. Historically, when a government begins to exert excessive control over the people and the people's rights are diminished, the government continues to expand its control and becomes totalitarian. Think of the pre-World War II advances of the Nazi government that Hitler and his henchmen ruled over. The government slowly exerted more and more control economically, educationally, and socially over the German people. It took years for the government to establish ultimate control over the people, and years afterward to undo.

On the other hand, when the government loses all control, chaos ensues. Think about the current situation regarding what is considered a minor crime or illegal immigration into the United States. The government in many areas has loosened laws on criminal behavior to a point where there is no fear of consequences for prohibited or criminal activity. Be it theft, assault, public indecency, or other acts, there is no legal consequence for improper behavior. If a person is arrested by police for certain crimes, there is no criminal prosecution initiated and, therefore no consequence. If a person is arrested in some states, such as Illinois, that person is released without posting bail and is scheduled for a future court date, only not to appear and again suffer no consequences. For a person who illegally enters the country, no consequences, no removal, and no return to their homeland. That person is released into the country with a promise to appear for a court hearing many months, or years later.

In the meantime, that person lives in the United States, uses the hospitals and emergency rooms for their medical needs, uses the community schools to educate their children, and uses community resources for housing and food services. There is no consequence for the improper behavior of entering the country without following the legally prescribed procedures therefore encouraging others to participate in this same behavior. With no control, the government ceases to function and the society faces anarchy and collapse. This also creates an environment where the citizens may take the law into their own hands. Just as it was in the old west and the wild frontier days of the mid to late 1800s.

The law enforcement officer sees their work as unimportant, ineffective, and worthless in this dysfunctional government. Why exert effort and time to pursue a criminal actor if that person will only be released before that officer can complete the reports? If a police officer sees a criminal act, why attempt to stop that act when the act will not result in any form of penalty under the law? When an officer faces the choice between possibly being harmed during an encounter or not having the encounter, why engage and face possible injury or legal consequences against themselves? As the law enforcement officer retreats, the government decline accelerates, moving the society closer to anarchy and collapse. Society and culture rely upon social norms, laws, and reasonable expectations of behavior to continue and advance. What happens when all of these are suddenly removed?

Chapter 18
Disrespected, Dishonored, and Under Assault

Throughout this same period, the nation has also experienced a loss of decorum, respect for others and their property, and a loss of the general sense of social norms. Some of these declines are related to the general decline in responsibility for improper or criminal behavior. Some of the declines are in the air of anonymity granted through the use of social media platforms and the internet. Some of the declines are out of a moral sense of righteous entitlement for perceived wrongs made by others against a person, or their historical heritage. Some of the declines are out of an organized effort to create chaos and discord in society. And some, are intentional acts, enacted out of a planned effort to create an environment for violent revolution within the society. All of these have led to changes in our culture and society.

As far as our first and most basic right granted to us under the First Amendment to the Constitution is the Right to Free Speech. During and following the very contentious and divisive presidential election of 2016 between Donald Trump and Hillary Rodham Clinton the country experienced a great increase in what amounts to 'silencing' of a person's right to free speech. During the election cycle, both candidates participated in what amounted to personal insults and name-calling, not only of the candidates but of their supporters as well. There were many insults and derogatory terms used to describe citizens of the country, based upon their political leanings. The terms used became pseudonyms which were used in the media as well. The use of the terms became commonplace and acceptable when referring to the political opposition.

One of the fallouts from this was the intentional disruption and 'silencing' of persons with a different political or social position. The term canceling became commonplace when referring to this action. Historically, the term blacklisting has been used to refer to this, which generally meant preventing a person from obtaining work in an industry, city, or region of the country, following some offense or perceived insult. In 2016 and 2017, the act of canceling a person or company, because of their political or social beliefs, gained popularity and use.

Especially targeted were speakers at colleges and universities in the United States. Statistically, more conservative-leaning speakers were targeted for this 'canceling', but it did happen to some progressive-leaning persons as well. Many of these incidents involved student activist groups who lobbied the school to either cancel a planned speaker's event or organize loud and raucous protests against the speaker during the event making it so they couldn't communicate their message or stance on a topic. Many of these protests involved so-called 'anti-fascist' groups blocking discussions and other events that were planned to discuss and cover topics such as free speech, racial issues, crime and enforcement, and conservative student group meetings. In most cases, the agitators and protestors were never disciplined by the school or arrested for their offenses, such as trespass or public disruption. The universities actually went so far as to voice support for the protestors saying they were engaged in protected speech under the First Amendment, which they were intentionally preventing others from exercising during planned events. In one case, a speaker was arrested for voicing their views, even though they were invited to speak by the university.

Other acts of 'canceling' targeted representatives of the Trump administration's Cabinet and administration. The Press Secretary for the Trump Administration was asked to leave a small family restaurant in Virginia because she worked for the Trump Administration and the employees didn't like the administration's policies on immigration. A cabinet official was booed and heckled by protestors inside a Washington, D.C. restaurant over border security policy decisions. Especially notable were comments made by Maxine Watters, a California Democrat Congresswoman, in June of 2018. Watters urged supporters 'if you see anybody from [Trump's] cabinet in a restaurant, in a department store, at a gasoline station, you get out and you create a crowd, and you push back on them, and you tell them they're not welcome anymore, anywhere'.

A resolution to censure Congresswoman Watters' comments was introduced in the House of Representatives citing that her comments were 'dangerous' and could lead to violence against persons. It was defeated in a 216-210 vote along party lines. Shortly after Congresswoman Watters' comments, several incidents occurred in which conservative-leaning persons were surrounded by progressive activists. The conservatives were heckled and threatened, and in some unfortunate cases, their property was vandalized and damaged and actual personal injury was caused to the conservative person.

The acts of disruption and public displays of defiance continued to grow along with the racial tensions as additional cases of possible excessive use of force by police occurred. In the midsummer of 2019 in New York City, New York Police Department (NYPD) Officers became the target of this disorder. On 22 July, two police officers were making an arrest of a subject when the video showed several people running up and dumping buckets of water on the police officers. The police officers, engaged with the subject trying to put them in the vehicle, but could not respond. Shortly thereafter another bucket is dumped on the officers and then as the person is backing away from the officers they throw the empty bucket, striking one of the officers in the head.

Over the next several days, additional disrespectful assaults involving drenching of NYPD officers with water would occur. Although the New York Mayor, Bill de Blasio, called the assaults 'unacceptable' and said the incidents were being investigated, only one person was ever charged with minor violations related to the initial incident. It is notable that these incidents occurred after the Eric Garner death investigations had ended with no criminal charges against the officers involved. The prevailing public opinion persisted that Eric Garner had died of an improper 'chokehold' used by the officer during Garner's arrest. The NYPD Commissioner praised his officers for their restraint in not reacting to these assaults but cautioned that the acts were 'dangerous' and could result in increased violence against police officers.

The effects of these public displays of disrespect and dishonor against police officers were spread across the country through media sources. Although the officers exercised restraint by not reacting, the acts showed a definite decrease in the public perception of police officers. Witnessing the officers, experiencing the disgrace of a virtual public 'tar and feathering', only served to further diminish the public respect for police authority. It also served to send a message to law enforcement officers across the country, that you are not respected in person, or as a profession. This was another blow to the already damaged morale of law enforcement across the country.

The Federal Bureau of Investigations (FBI) maintains records of the number of law enforcement officers assaulted and killed in the line of duty each year. They publish this information in the Uniform Crime Reporting (UCR) Program where they break down the numbers based on whether the officer was killed by a felonious act, a crime, or because of an accident, such as a motor vehicle crash or other accidental causation. The UCR also displays the number of officers assaulted and the number of reported injuries resulting from those assaults. The method of assault may range from a personal weapon, a fist, to a weapon such as a gun, knife, or other object. Below are charts summarizing the data.

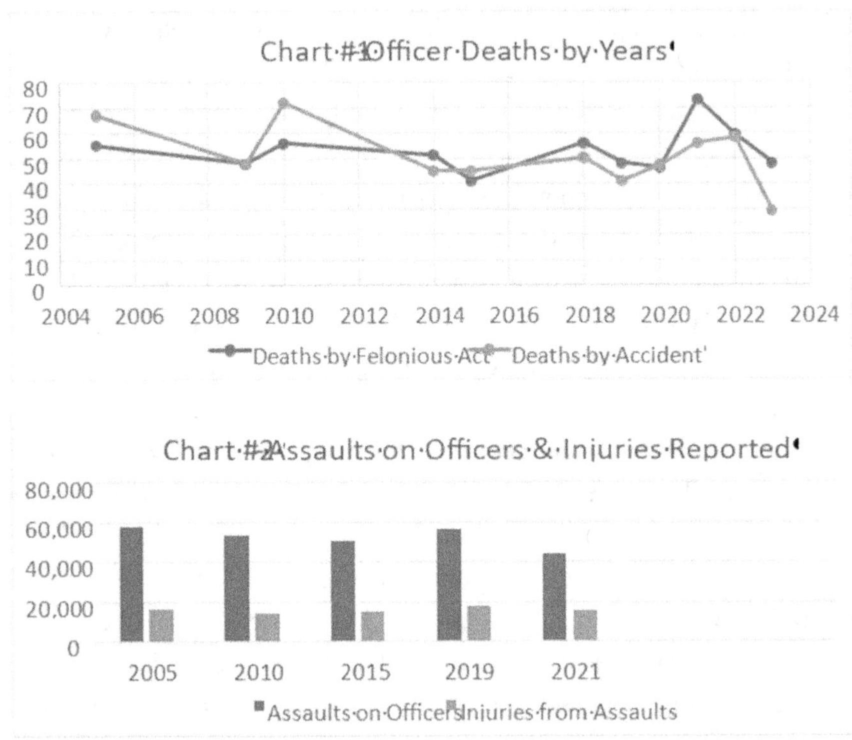

In Chart #1 above, you notice a large spike (59% increase) in officer felonious act-related deaths in 2021 which correlates to the timeframe of the post-2020 widespread civil unrest and the calls to defund police departments. During that year, the number of ambush-style attacks on officers doubled in frequency. This correlates to the time when police departments were experiencing increased pressure to use restraint when dealing with persons of minority descent because of repeated high-profile cases involving the use of force. Law enforcement officers were facing not only external public pressure but also internal departmental pressure, to moderate their responses to avoid possible liability during encounters with the public. The law enforcement officers found themselves on the defensive having to explain every action taken during encounters with the public.

The term 'de-escalation' became a catch phrase used by departmental management and was inserted into training programs to try to reduce the potential of increased levels of force used during encounters. Unfortunately, the sudden change in techniques and attitudes resulted in more hesitation by law enforcement officers during encounters, putting them at a disadvantage in vulnerable situations. This new method of dealing with persons in critical situations takes time to incorporate into the everyday mindset of officers with long-term experience and service. The mantra of de-escalation was imprinted upon officers at every opportunity and the officer was expected to immediately accept this and implement it. The implementation of this training created additional risk for officers as they now had to take time to consider how they would deal with the encounter under the new initiative and policy of de-escalation. During any critical situation, the loss of time because of a delay in action or hesitation to act significantly increases the risk to the officer or others.

Another issue that relates to law enforcement officer deaths and assaults is the public perception regarding mental health issues. In many cases, police are called to assist during mental health crisis-type events. In most cases, police officers receive very little training in dealing with a subject who is experiencing a mental health crisis. Mental health crisis' may involve any number of situations including persons who have been previously diagnosed with a mental health disorder and controls their medical condition with medication. There are also situations where substance abuse, be it alcohol or other intoxicant, is being used by the person putting them in an intentionally, or unintentionally altered mental state. Another situation that officers commonly encounter is persons threatening self-harm or suicide, especially situations involving weapons.

There is a multitude of other situations which may fall within the mental health crisis category as well. In most of these cases, police officers are called in to attempt to mitigate the mental health crisis. Law enforcement officers are not specifically trained for these situations and have limited tools available to them to handle these situations. The officer finds themselves on the scene dealing with a situation they may have never encountered before. The situation may sometimes be highly emotional, not only by the subject in crisis but also by family or friends seeking help for themselves and the subject. When there are weapons or potential harm threatened to others, officers find themselves between their duty to assist the subject and to protect themselves and others from the potential threat. The situations often become a 'lose, lose' situation for the officers, caught between the conflicting interests. The officers, with limited mental health training and resources, have to find a way on their own to navigate through these encounters. These types of situations put the officer at a major disadvantage as they try to resolve these events, without relying upon their training and experience.

Ultimately, law enforcement officers are people who have all the fragility and problems of every other person in the community. They have families, including spouses and children. They have friends and relatives, parents, siblings, and people they associate with. Some may have served in the military prior to entering the law enforcement career, continuing a spirit of service to the country and community through the law enforcement career. Others enter the law enforcement profession through family tradition, following in the footsteps of their parent or other family members to serve the community. Overwhelmingly, law enforcement officers enter the profession through the calling of duty to serve their communities and the people in them.

The law enforcement profession is very similar to the military in that officers may learn information about people and places within their communities that they cannot readily share outside law enforcement circles. At times, this can cause conflicts outside the work environment with friends and family. This can also lead to a closing of the circle of friends for the law enforcement officer, reducing their outside contacts. Over time, the law enforcement professional can become isolated and tends only to socialize with other members of the law enforcement community. This can lead the officer to narrow their point of view and see everything and everyone from a law enforcement point of view.

Law enforcement officers get to see the human condition in all its disorder and ugliness. The law enforcement officer responds to natural disasters and works through inclement weather and dangerous situations. They respond to accidents of all kinds including household injuries, fires, and vehicle accidents. Of course, they respond to various reports of criminal activity and mental health crises. Most officers have first responder training and are the first to respond and render aid to injured persons, in cases of multiple injuries, they perform triage on the victims. In some cases, officers are the first to discover persons who have died, whether from natural causes or otherwise. In cases of criminal violence, the law enforcement officer must act to preserve evidence while still treating the victim medically, or with respect owed to a deceased person. At times, it is the officer who delivers unfortunate news of the untimely death of a loved one to the family. The law enforcement officer experiences all of this and is expected to continue to be a contributing member of their family, community, and department.

Some are unable to cope with the experiences of the job. Officers tend to internalize any concerns that may develop because of these experiences, hiding the symptoms of developing problems. Sometimes officers may use alcohol or other substances to self-medicate for the problems, covering the symptoms with a machismo which is traditional within the profession. Officers share drinks with each other and talk among themselves, either after their shifts or at social gatherings, which are attended by primarily other law enforcement officers, developing an unhealthy closed coping system.

The concealed underlying problems often result in self-destructive behavior which can lead to family discord, financial problems, or ultimately suicide. Suicide rates among law enforcement officers traditionally exceed the national average by up to four times in frequency. In 2019, a reported 228 officers committed suicide, the highest on record. Those losses more than doubled the number of officers killed in the line of duty by accident and criminal acts combined. In 2022, the Federal Bureau of Investigation began requesting departments report officer suicides in the Uniform Crime Reporting data so the Department of Justice can start studying officers' suicide causations and develop programs to address the rising epidemic within the profession.

Because of all the perceived and actual issues within the law enforcement profession, the profession has experienced a significant decline in not only active members but also a decline in popularity among persons seeking professions. Throughout many departments, officers have left, through retirement or quitting the profession. The reasons are varied but the personnel losses affect departments of all sizes, from small to large. In Goodhue,

Minnesota, the entire police department resigned over poor pay in August 2023. The Police Chief and all seven officers resigned leaving the small town without police services for most of that day. The small town council had to quickly contract with the county sheriff department to perform law enforcement services in the town. This is an extreme example, but many large city police departments have experienced significant reductions in size, namely Minneapolis, Seattle, Chicago, and Portland. The situation has not improved as hiring and replacing lost officers remains difficult because of negative public perception and government compensation packages lagging the private sector offerings.

Chapter 19
Reforms to Consider

So, what happens now to heal the wounds and save the law enforcement profession? This is not the first, nor probably the last time, that law enforcement will need to change with the culture and society. The last major change occurred after the civil rights movement and the anti-Vietnam War period. There were reforms that were being implemented during the pre-911 period, however, the events of that day halted those changes and prevented them from taking hold. The Great Recession of 2008 caused such financial destruction in governmental entities that police departments and the law enforcement profession suffered significantly. Following the Recession, the excessive use of force cases that we explored in previous chapters occurred, bringing additional pressure upon governmental entities and police departments. All these factors culminated in the political and social calls to defund police departments across the country that we are now hearing. Because of the defunding, decreasing staffing, and demoralization of police departments and officers, our society is experiencing a rise in crime which has not happened in many decades.

The increase in crime is also affecting our communities and culture as retailers and the citizenry react to that crime. Many retailers have closed stores in areas targeted by crime due to repeated losses. Major national chains such as pharmacies, big-box retailers, and designer retailers have been severely affected by the increased crime, usually well-organized and targeted at certain products which easily resell. Many small businesses have closed or moved out of neighborhoods, even those owned by community members. This results in the loss of services and availability of goods within the neighborhood. The community members must go elsewhere for goods and services, causing a loss of vitality in the neighborhood. The decline may begin the vicious circle of neighborhood loss, increasing the decline. As neighborhoods lose access to goods and services, community members leave causing yet more loss of neighborhood stability and vitality.

We must identify areas where reforms can be implemented that will begin to reverse the negative societal perception of law enforcement. To do this we must openly and honestly critique where we have been, what has happened, and where we want to go in the future. Only once the areas have been identified and plans have been made can we hope to reverse the losses in the profession. The process will not be quick or without its failures, but somehow the discussion must be started before society becomes too stricken with disorder and chaos.

Several possible areas of reform include hiring and retention of personnel, re-evaluating and updating training programs and techniques, refreshing and reintroducing community policing models, and protecting the criminal justice system from possible political influence. These are not by any means the only places where reforms can be implemented, they are just starting points to address identified problem areas. Of course, racial bias should be addressed not only within law enforcement departments but also within the greater governmental structure such as community leadership and the court system.

When it comes to the hiring of law enforcement officers by a governmental entity, there is no consistency across cities, counties, states, or even within the federal government. Each state establishes a Police Officer Standards and Training (P.O.S.T.) Commission which establishes the qualifications for law enforcement hiring and retention within that individual state. The states have varying levels of qualification, but all require some basic minimums. They relate to citizenship, not only to be a citizen of the United States or in some cases, a Legally Admitted Permanent Resident (LAPR) in the citizenship process, but also sometimes to be a resident of the community in which they work. Minimum age requirements of at least 18 years of age, but most require a candidate to be 21 years old. There are also maximum age limits in some positions which vary by agency or department. Educational requirements of at a minimum a High School diploma or High School Graduation Equivalent Degree (GED) where some states and agencies require two-year or four-year college degrees. Candidates must have a valid driver's license or be able to obtain one prior to beginning training. Because of the physical nature of the position there are also physical fitness requirements which vary by department or agency.

The P.O.S.T. boards also establish what factors may disqualify a person from seeking a law enforcement position. Common disqualifiers are past conviction of a felony offense, past conviction of misdemeanor domestic violence, sexual violations, or perjury. Other disqualifying conditions may be lack of physical fitness, unable to pass written tests, poor credit history, dishonorable discharge from military service, falsification of information on an application, poor driving history or alcohol violation, past illegal drug use, past involvement in organized gang activity, and racial bias exhibited by a candidate. These factors are open to interpretation by the hiring entity based upon a case-by-case basis.

Each state sets its own qualifications, and the state may establish stricter guidelines for officers in that state. Some additional qualifications may include medical training at the first responder level, continuing educational requirements of varying degrees and lengths, and completion of a training standards academy. Individual departments may set standards as well including completion of a departmental training academy.

The standards that are set by state P.O.S.T. commissions are supposed to ensure that law enforcement officers within the state all meet basic and equal standards however, there is a great disparity from state to state. This disparity may be readily apparent when jurisdictions meet at a state line and the two states have greatly varied qualification standards. Comparing the minimum requirements for the states of Washington and Oregon several differences are apparent. In Washington, a person must be 18 years of age, in Oregon, 21. In Washington, a person must not have a criminal record, in Oregon; the person must have a 'clean' criminal record with no felonies of any kind. In Washington, a person must possess a valid Washington driver's license, in Oregon, you must have a good driving record or be able to acquire a valid driver's license prior to hiring. Both states require a candidate to be a United States citizen, but Oregon requires documentation to verify that status. Oregon has a requirement to be of good moral character and good health, Washington has no such requirement. From this brief comparison, one can see how the differences between neighboring states may lead to problems. For example, the legal drinking age in Washington is 21 years of age, but a police officer can be certified to enforce those laws at the age of 18.

In light of the disparities between states and their differing P.O.S.T. requirements, I mention a few possible updates to the basic requirements for law enforcement officers through the P.O.S.T. Commission System. First, the minimum age of candidates should be set to equal the legal drinking age of the state. This only seems reasonable. Secondly, add a requirement that candidates undergo an in-person interview with a panel of licensed officers representing the department or entity to which they have applied or been offered a position. There is no better way to assess a candidate's ability to perform the job than an in-person interview. The interview should be structured to challenge the candidate to handle one or two scenarios they may encounter during their profession. Experienced officers who have been trained to conduct these interviews would be capable of assessing the candidate's ability to handle the situations in a professional, safe, and reasonable manner. In my career, I have conducted thousands of these types of interviews, and I found it is a very effective way of determining which candidates are most ready to perform the job. The candidate usually experiences a small bit of stress during these types of interviews. The stress reveals the candidate's thought processes and ability to prioritize critical actions necessary to resolve a scenario.

Finally, add a requirement that each state would administer a psychological evaluation of candidates. Not necessarily to determine just mental fitness for the profession, but also to provide a baseline for future evaluations if needed. Law enforcement officers see much of the negative side of society and unfortunately, some of the worst things in society. They are also exposed to significant risks of injury. Not unlike an athlete or a soldier in the military, those risks represent increased potential for physical and mental injuries or disorders. Providing a baseline for comparison after possible future evaluations will improve the ability to explain, mitigate, and treat those risks.

The P.O.S.T requirements, or a state's equivalent board or commission, are an existing system that all states currently use. This means it wouldn't require any additional governmental influence or intervention, just a simple update of the currently accepted minimum requirements. These suggestions are most likely already being utilized at departments across the country so updating the requirements only reinforces these procedures.

When it comes to re-evaluating and updating training programs and techniques, it is a common and ever-evolving thing in law enforcement. New equipment is commonly integrated into use which makes the profession more efficient, such as in squad computer systems. A new piece of equipment such as an electronic control device (ECD), referred to as a Taser in common language, is intended to increase options for officers to engage with subjects in a safe and effective manner causing the least harm. When new equipment is introduced, departmental policies regarding use and the reporting requirements should be updated as well. This clearly establishes the guidelines for the law enforcement officer and the criminal justice system to determine whether the use is justifiable on a case-by-case basis.

In December 2014, following the shooting death of Michael Brown, the Obama administration announced a Department of Justice grant program providing funds for departments to obtain body-worn cameras for their officers. The cameras would provide video and audio evidence of police and citizen encounters for use in court and when complaints of excessive force or other misconduct may have occurred. Although many departments were equipped, there were many that were not, especially in the federal law enforcement system. There is also a wide range of regulations concerning their use by departments and certain units within departments. As determined in the Breonna Taylor shooting case in March 2020, although the plainclothes officers had body-worn cameras issued to them, there were no regulations requiring the officers to wear and activate those devices during warrant services. The lack of their use during the incident meant no video evidence was available during the investigation to compare to forensic evidence obtained after the incident. Following Breonna Taylor's death, the Kentucky legislature acted to establish state law requiring the use of body-worn cameras and setting parameters for their use during investigative warrant service in the future.

When it comes to new equipment, such as body-worn cameras, there are additional legal and technical concerns as well. First, a person's privacy rights and the rights of others who may or may not be involved, especially when being recorded. Another issue is the data storage requirements for maintaining the downloaded camera data. How long must a department hold onto the data? What storage needs and recovery systems are necessary for the data, and its protection from unauthorized access?

Ongoing review of training programs and authorized equipment also involves maintaining a cadre of trained persons capable of sharing that knowledge with other officers. The training officers need to regularly update their training processes to remain current with new and evolving tactics and procedures. Once a law enforcement officer completes basic training and is assigned patrol duties, the training must continue throughout their career. This involves not only equipment but also tactics, techniques, and legal decisions that may affect the officer in their position. Typically, officers who are new to the position or a department are teamed with an experienced officer to guide them in the early months of their careers. The training officer is expected to guide the new officer to gain the experience and knowledge necessary for their duties. Those training officers must be re-evaluated as to their capabilities to impart relevant and current training to reinforce the training from the academy or other training programs that the department utilizes. Officer Chauvin, who knelt on George Floyd to control him without regard to Floyd's safety and health was a training officer, field training the three officers who were also involved in the George Floyd case. A department must be cognizant of who is training new officers and what those officers are teaching new personnel.

One possible training technique that I would be interested to see if it could be incorporated into the officer training program would be the use of simulators or virtual reality headsets. Although simulators have been around for some time, the frequency of their availability to law enforcement for training is minimal. A simulator allows an officer to 'experience' a multitude of different situations in a safe and controlled manner. It gives them the ability to learn how to work through common and uncommon situations without presenting a risk to them or the public. The officer could make a mistake and learn from that mistake without anyone being injured or creating liability for the officer or department. The use of the new virtual reality headsets could make this form of training available to many departments without significant investment in equipment, space, and technology.

Currently, available police 'shoot, don't shoot' simulator programs could be modified and expanded through virtual reality systems to incorporate a multitude of potential police encounters. Officers could experience vehicle pursuits in all types of weather and environments from rural to urban. Officers could experience traffic stops with a multitude of different outcomes, from unremarkable to critical incidents. Officers could experience encounters with pedestrians that range from simple investigative interviews to armed encounters to mental health crises. The training options are limitless. At a significant cost savings of actual live training involving modified equipment and warehouses full of vehicles, actors or role-players, props, costumes, and training environment rooms. This form of training would also reduce accidental injuries suffered during training exercises, good for both the department and the officer. If commercial airlines can train pilots to fly passenger airplanes, astronauts can navigate space and a weightless environment, and the military can train soldiers to operate sophisticated technology like tanks and other devices on simulators, why can't our law enforcement community utilize these technologies as well?

In training, nothing can replace the real thing. However, the use of virtual reality can safely and inexpensively provide a means to allow officers to gain knowledge and experience, which may help them should they face something similar in the field. Replicating the encounters and causing a person's body to react by inducing stress and incorporating decision-making into the training environment. Virtual reality may provide a means for the officer to make a mistake and learn from it, without causing anyone harm. With an estimated 18,000–20,000 law enforcement entities in the United States of various sizes, the acquisition of the training equipment would be a minimal investment. A corporate partner could further reduce the expense and provide the necessary technology to maintain and update training software. The Department of Justice could fund this through a grant initiative like the Obama administration-funded body-worn cameras. The DOJ could oversee the development of training scenarios with input from law enforcement training experts.

Over the course of the last several decades, law enforcement officers have increasingly become separated from the community that they serve. With repeated incidents of apparent excessive use of force which happened between 2013 and 2020, the separation increased. Following the deaths of Breonna Taylor and George Floyd in 2020 calls for defunding police departments grew increasingly persuasive politically. Many major city community leaders responded to the calls and severely cut police department budgets. This was just as those same police departments finally began to recover their personnel numbers back to pre-2008 'Great Recession' levels. The civil disorder and protests that persisted throughout the summer of 2020 further strained police departments and their personnel. With the pressures and the lack of public and political support, many police personnel opted to retire or simply quit and sought another career outside policing. The same pressures that led to the personnel losses also created an environment that severely affected the recruitment of new candidates into the law enforcement profession to replace the losses. After the summer of protests and demonstrations, the economy suffered a severe blow because of the COVID-19 pandemic and efforts taken to minimize the disease spread and contagion.

Now, with the increase in criminal activity and many departments still severely short of personnel, the departments are struggling to fill vacancies in their ranks. It may seem counterintuitive, but this may be the right time to reintroduce the Community Policing Model which was starting to be more prevalent before the 9/11 terrorist attacks changed everything. The Community Policing Model is based on building trust and communication with the public, residents, private businesses, and schools within the community to perform police functions. This model emphasizes service and support within the community, not over-policing the community. The Community Policing Model may serve multiple benefits at this time of negative public perception of law enforcement.

Starting with the businesses and residents that may be affected by increased crime in the community the Community Policing Model would engage police with the person most affected by that activity. By engaging in community forums and educational presentations the police department may be able to build new and strengthen existing, relationships. By re-engaging with schools and the community youth, the police department could promote anti-crime and anti-drug use programs and build trust within the community youth. At one time, youth were encouraged to seek out a police officer if they were lost, scared, or felt unsure about something or someone. Now, youth are being instructed to fear and distrust the police because the police are the 'bad guys' who are only trying to hurt you or arrest you or your family members. What a horrible thing to teach our youth. Another benefit of engaging youth is that police officers can learn the popular slang and common social media 'hot topics', which may help to reduce disputes and common misunderstandings during field encounters. Community Policing Models have the added benefit that the community becomes invested in anti-crime efforts through neighborhood watches, community efforts to reduce drug use and encourage more involvement in crisis situations, such as natural disasters.

One additional benefit that may develop through the Community Policing Model is an overall improvement in the reputation and public perception of law enforcement officers and their departments. This improved public perception will hopefully encourage new candidates to seek out the profession, to 'serve and protect' their community. A new generation of officers with a new perception of policing may lead to increased interest in the career helping to alleviate the personnel losses suffered over the last several years.

Early on, we discussed the criminal justice system and the various components that exist within the system. Law enforcement officers working patrol duties were described as the most visible part of that system but are only a small part of the overall system. Our form of government, a Representative Republic, relies upon an orderly and engaged society in which to function. The criminal justice system which involves our police forces, our courts, and our correctional services, requires all the parts to work cohesively together to maintain societal norms and values. When one part of the system fails, the whole system is at risk of failure, resulting in chaos and disorder in society.

Chapters 2 and 3 covered the United States Constitution, the 10th Amendment to the Constitution, and the criminal justice system extensively. Within those chapters, we learned what the responsibilities and capabilities of the branches of government are, and what their limitations are. We also learned how their power to create and enforce laws is derived from the people and how those laws may be changed as society changes. We discovered how the different components of the criminal justice system work together, as if spokes in a wheel, to keep order, justice, and fairness in a large and diverse population spread across the continent.

Within that system, we find sub-systems of the federal, state, county, municipal, and local levels. All those systems are built upon a common frame with specific jurisdictions, powers, and responsibilities.

The one thing we didn't cover is how the people, the citizens, choose the representatives in that criminal justice system. This process is just as critical to the proper function of the criminal justice system as any rule, regulation, or Article of the Constitution. It is, after all, the people within the system that make the system function. In the federal Court system, the President nominates persons for the United States Supreme Court, and in the lesser Courts, the Senate vets the nominees and either approves or disapproves the appointments. The Attorney General of the United States, who serves as the leader of the Department of Justice (DOJ), is a cabinet-level position and that person is appointed by the President to serve at the President's privilege with the advice and consent of the Senate. In the state system, filling positions within the criminal justice system has been left to the legislative branch of the individual states to determine how those positions get filled. In most states, the people elect their Supreme Court Justices, District Court Judges, and State Attorney Generals during regularly scheduled elections within the states.

When it comes to the federal court system with the President being re-elected every four years, the Attorney General and the direction of the Department of Justice will tend to lean in whatever direction the President does politically. The DOJ is expected to remain politically neutral but obviously, certain issues will tend to sway politically with the administration in power. As the President nominates Supreme Court Justices for lifetime terms, a President appointing a justice to the highest court in the land can affect the direction in which the Court may interpret the Constitution. Those appointments can last over a very long period and may cross-generational periods of society.

In the state system, the election process can present a vulnerability to the criminal justice system. As representatives are elected, the influence of money through direct campaign contributions, campaign support from political parties, and indirect support through Political Action Committees (PACs), or 'dark money' as it is commonly termed, can substantially influence election results. These sources of campaign financing can far outweigh the common citizens' financial contributions and therefore lessen the importance of the 'peoples' expressed interests and societal objectives.

As an example, during the 2022 Wisconsin Supreme Court race, an estimated $45,000,000.00 was spent during the campaigns. Both campaigns were funded by large donors making maximum donations to the individual campaigns and then massive donations through political parties and PACs. Between both candidates, approximately 28,800 persons contributed $50.00 or less to the campaigns for a total of about $700,000.00. Similarly, 61 persons contributed a maximum of $20,000.00 for a total of $1,240,000.00 to the campaigns. With that kind of contribution, those 61 persons will most likely get much more influence with the candidate than the small donors. The majority of the remaining $43,000,000.00 came from political parties and 'dark money' sources which will also exercise major influence over the candidate who prevails. Those sources generally have specific and determined agendas and don't represent the majority of society or their common interests. This form of influence can certainly affect the direction of the Supreme Court in Wisconsin for possibly decades to come. This may result in the citizens of the state living under the beliefs and desires of the few, or the undisclosed contributors, who supported the candidate.

In other political races such as for county judge and county or state attorney general, the influence of election campaign donations can similarly affect the citizens of a state disproportionately. If a state attorney general or county attorney serving as the lead prosecutor for that governmental entity does not enforce laws duly enacted by the legislature, the law is rendered moot and ineffective. This has been evidenced in several large cities in the United States over the past several years, especially in California and Illinois. California has experienced a significant increase in retail theft as the state has increased the dollar amount of goods stolen before a criminal prosecution can be considered to a point where the theft is unable to be prosecuted in court. County prosecutors in California have also reduced the frequency of criminal prosecution for many offenses, effectively making those laws moot as the actor is not charged for the offense. In Illinois, the state recently instituted a legislative change to eliminate bail, the payment of a financial bond prior to release from jail, for most minor and mid-level offenses. If a criminal actor is arrested for any of these qualifying offenses, they are immediately released from custody following initial processing, set with a court date in the future. There are no repercussions for the criminal act and the offender is soon freed from police custody, usually before the arresting officer has completed their shift and the required arrest reporting paperwork.

Our criminal justice system is critical for the orderly and just function of our society. Our culture, built on the principles of freedom, justice, fairness, and the democratic process, is at risk of descent into chaos and anarchy. The people through an appropriate legislative process should consider how to protect our criminal justice system from the influence of financial contributions to these critical positions within the criminal justice system. If changes aren't considered, the criminal justice system may revert to the time of 'the American Old West', when justice was meted out by vigilantes, with a gun and a rope. The law was determined and enforced by a limited number of persons, **over** the majority, based upon what benefited the few who wielded financial and political influence and power.

At the outset of this effort, the author set forth the idea that the law enforcement profession was declining and was in serious threat of continued decline without reform. The profession faced pressure from multiple sources including political, social, and financial influencing the decline. It is hoped that in exploring this effort, the reader was able to gain insight into not only the law enforcement profession but also the government and its organizational structure that creates the necessity for law enforcement. The reader has gained an understanding of how law enforcement historically developed and what factors played into the changes that occurred within law enforcement over time. Understanding history is a large part of understanding the society and culture that determine the direction of law enforcement in the United States. Major events and incidents that have occurred in the recent past affected the law enforcement profession and how it is perceived and functions at this time.

Understanding where the profession has come from, what the expectations are, what societal and cultural forces affect it, and what deficiencies it may have, will allow society to look to make reasonable and acceptable changes in the future. The conversation must begin with truth and understanding, without which no conclusion can be reached. If both sides remain stoic and set in their ways, no progress can be made. Progress will require change and reform, which won't be the first or last time for the law enforcement profession. Society and culture will continue to evolve and change, the law enforcement officer will have to evolve and change with it.

All of us must be involved in the solution. Our society and culture depend upon it, and our law enforcement personnel deserve it.